Primary ICT and the Foundation Subjects

Also available from Continuum

Primary ICT and the Foundation Subjects

John Williams and Nick Easingwood

continuum

In memory of John Williams
Teacher, mentor and friend
1936–2006

Since this book was completed in the summer of 2006,
John Williams has sadly died.
This book is dedicated to him and to his memory.

Continuum International Publishing Group

The Tower Building   80 Maiden Lane, Suite 704
11 York Road   New York
London SE1 7NX   NY 10038

www.continuumbooks.com

British Library Cataloguing-in-Publication Data
A catalogue record for this book is available from the British Library.

ISBN: 0826490395 (paperback)

Typeset by Ben Cracknell Studios | www.benstudios.co.uk

Printed and bound in Great Britain by The Cromwell Press, Trowbridge, Wiltshire

Contents

Acknowledgements

We would particularly like to thank the staff and children of the following schools for the help, co-operation and hospitality shown by them during the writing of this book: Karen Smith and Ian Watson of Kenningtons Primary School, Aveley, Thurrock; Paul Edwards and Class 5 of Tewin Cowper Primary School, Hertfordshire; and Mrs Anne Goldsmith and her Year Six class at St Adrian's RC Primary School, St Albans, Hertfordshire.

Our thanks are also extended to Initial Teacher Training students of the Faculty of Education of Anglia Ruskin University, Chelmsford, Essex, with particular thanks to trainees Rachel Hiley and to Stephanie Wharton. The latter completed her placement at Collingwood Primary School, South Woodham Ferrers, Essex.

Addresses of Suppliers

2simple Software,
3–4 Sentinel Square,
Brent Street,
Hendon,
London,
NW4 2EL
www.2simple.com

AVP
School Hill Centre,
Chepstow,
Monmouthshire,
NP16 5PH

Commotion Group,
Unit 11, Tannery Road,
Tonbridge,
Kent,
TN9 1RF

Data Harvest Group Limited,
Woburn Lodge,
Waterloo Road,
Linslade,
Leighton Buzzard,
Bedfordshire,
LU7 7NR

Dial Solutions,
PO Box 84,
Leeds,
LS15 8UZ

Flexible Software Ltd,
PO Box 100,
Abingdon,
Oxon,
OX13 6PQ

Focus Educational Software Ltd,
PO Box 52,
Truro,
Cornwall,
TR1 1ZJ
www.focuseducational.com

Granada Learning Ltd
(Black Cat),
Granada Television,
Quay Street,
Manchester,
M60 9EA

Keep I.T. Easy,
P.O. Box 29,
Nuneaton,
Warwickshire,
CV11 4TT

Lego Robolab (see details for Commotion)

Logotron Ltd,
124 Cambridge Science Park,
Milton Road,
Cambridge,
CB4 0ZS

Microsoft UK,
Microsoft Campus,
Thames Valley Park,
Reading,
RG6 1WG

Promethean Ltd,
TDS House,
Lower Philips Road,
Blackburn,
Lancashire,
BB1 5TH

Softease,
Market Place,
Ashbourne,
Derbyshire,
DE6 1ES

Valiant Technology,
Valiant House,
3 Grange Mills,
Weir Road,
London,
SW12 0NE

Virtual Language Systems Ltd,
Park House,
5 Park Road,
Chorley,
Lancashire,
PR7 1QU
www.vls-onlineschool.com

Figure Credits

- Screenshots reprinted by permission from Microsoft Corporation. Microsoft is a trademark of the Microsoft Corporation.
- Figures 1.1, 2.3, 2.4, 3.8, 3.9, 3.10, 3.12, 3.13, 3.14, and 3.15 by Nick Easingwood
- Figures 1.2, 1.3, 1.4, 1.5, 1.6 and 1.7 by Stephanie Wharton
- Figures 2.1, 2.2, 2.5, 3.6, 3.7, 5.1, 6.1 and 6.2 by John Williams
- Figure 2.6 by Keep IT Simple – Flowol
- Figure 2.7 by Bee Bot
- All photographs by Nick Easingwood except for Figures 2.8, 4.1, 4.2 (Data Harvest), 3.1 and 3.2 (Kenningtons School, Aveley)
- Figures 3.3, 3.4, 3.5 by Rachel Hiley
- Figures 3.11, 6.7, 6.8, 7.1, 7.2, 7.3 and 8.1 by Promethean
- Figures 3.16, 3.17, 3.18, 3.19, 3.20 and 4.6 by 2Simple
- Figures 4.3, 4.4 and 4.5 by Data Harvest
- Figures 5.2 and 5.3 by Tewin School
- Figures 6.3, 6.4, 6.5, 6.6 by St. Adrians RC School
- Figure 7.4 by Granada – Fresco

Foreword

'Education, education, education' was the rallying cry of the British Prime Minister Tony Blair. Unfortunately, education as a creative and interactive process has often been sidetracked, with the emphasis on 'teaching' and 'learning' as if they constituted completely separate processes – the implication being that the child's mind is simply a container for knowledge that is already pre-packaged. Equally, true education in schools has been hampered by an obsession with testing and examinations, with an increasingly narrow focus on the so-called 'three R's' (literacy and numeracy) to the neglect of a more comprehensive education, and with the barrage of 'initiatives' and demands from a centralized state bureaucracy – demands that tend to serve the needs of control and administration rather than of education.

What is salutary about John Williams' and Nick Easingwood's book *Primary ICT and the Foundation Subjects* is that it makes a strong plea for a comprehensive, child-centred form of education. It thus acknowledges that education is not only about the acquisition of knowledge, but must also involve and encourage the inherent creativity and thinking of the children themselves. Following the insights of the psychologist Edward De Bono, they emphasize the fact that the child actually 'enjoys thinking', and that the school curriculum and the planning of lessons must therefore be devised so as to encourage independent thinking and the child's inherent curiosity. They have already produced two excellent and user-friendly textbooks that have promoted and provided guidance for the use of ICT (information and communication technology) in the teaching of mathematics and science in primary schools. This book details how to use such technology in the teaching of the Foundation Subjects in primary schools.

After an initial chapter relating to the planning, preparation and execution of a typical lesson, the book contains chapters on each of the Foundation Subjects: design and technology, art and design, geography, history, music, modern foreign languages and even physical education. (Alas! The importance of the social sciences such as sociology and anthropology has yet to penetrate the cloisters of government.) What the authors stress throughout is the way that computers and other forms of communication technology can be utilized in an imaginative and creative way to enhance the Foundation Subjects (or forms of knowledge) while at the same time developing the child's own interests and capacity for independent thought.

Ever since Charles Snow wrote his famous essay on *The Two Cultures* (1959), in which he bewailed the fact that a deep chasm had emerged between literary intellectuals and the natural sciences, the danger of over-specialization has been recognized. (Snow, it is worth noting, was a research scientist as well as a successful novelist and talented administrator.) Even so, evolutionary biologists like Edward Wilson and Stephen Jay Gould are still pleading that there is a need for some form of 'consilience' that brings together the sciences and the humanities in a constructive way. John Williams and Nick Easingwood are motivated by a similar concern. They thus stress the need for a comprehensive education at the primary level, and they are critical of the undue emphasis on the core subjects. Young children, they suggest, have an inherent curiosity: they are eager to learn, and have the capacity to be interested in a wide range of subjects, activities and interests. Children actually enjoy thinking. It is important then, the authors argue, that children not only become proficient in numeracy and literacy but are also given a 'richer education' in which they learn to understand their local environment, as well as the society and the wider world in which they live. This entails a grounding in a wide range of subjects and perspectives. The authors of this text therefore emphasize and demonstrate the ways in which ICT can be imaginatively used to enhance the teaching and learning of the Foundation Subjects in primary schools. But they put an equal emphasis on the fact that ICT is an important skill and subject in its own right, and can be creatively used to establish linkages between subjects right across the curriculum.

ICT and the Foundation Subjects is full of insights, useful suggestions, practical ideas and lesson plans for teachers, mostly derived from the authors' own experiences. It is inspired by the need to re-affirm a comprehensive, child-centred education. I thus warmly recommend it to primary teachers.

Brian Morris B.Ed. Ph.D.
Emeritus Professor of Anthropology
Goldsmiths College, University of London

Introduction

A child enjoys thinking. Edward de Bono.

This book is about using ICT in its many forms – the computer, of course, but also through such additions as the digital camera and the interactive whiteboard – to support where relevant the teaching of the Foundation Subjects.

The Foundation Subjects

We have taken these to be those listed in the National Curriculum for England. They are all subjects likely to be found in any broad-based curriculum.

They are:

- Design and Technology
- Art and Design
- History
- Geography
- Modern Foreign Languages
- Music
- Physical Education

We have not included Personal, Social and Health Education (otherwise known as PSHE and Citizenship), because at the time of writing the contents of this subject are still under discussion. For those who are not conversant with the National Curriculum, it should be noted that English, Mathematics and Science are all part of it, but are treated separately as 'Core Subjects', and consequently often given precedence over the Foundation Subjects. We shall comment more about this later in the book.

What we hope to show is that all areas within the curriculum should also include the extra 'hidden subject', which is of course ICT. When it becomes an integral part of a pupil's daily activities, there are opportunities to enhance the learning of both the individual subject, and the skills needed for ICT. Moreover, if we are to teach a broad curriculum we can harness the ability of the computer and other forms of hardware to help remove the 'drudgery' of producing written lists and graphs, recorded facts and descriptions. All this can be done quickly and accurately with the use of suitable databases or spreadsheet programs, or by using other forms of technology such as the digital camera. In short, the use of ICT can help save time, time that can be given to actual teaching and learning. This development of what is known as ICT capability – that is, the knowledge, skills and understanding of when and when not (as well as how) to use ICT in a range of different subject and activity-based contexts – is crucial to the accessing of higher levels of learning.

Despite this, there are subjects that are taught without the use (or correct use) of ICT. It might be wrong, for example, to rely too much on CD-Roms when teaching history. This could even make this exciting subject boring. What we hope to show is how the proper and relevant use of all aspects of ICT can enhance both the teaching and learning of the Foundation Subjects for all. In this context it is interesting to note that for history, England's National Curriculum gives at least four directions for this use of ICT. We make no apologies for mentioning this document, which is after all statutory and must be followed by all schools in England. It is also far more flexible and interesting than many of the formal lesson plans used in many schools.

ICT and a broad-based curriculum

Before we look at the use of ICT across the curriculum in more detail, we should consider how such a cross-curricular approach could affect some aspects of our teaching, and even the structure of the curriculum itself. Such linking of subjects when teaching a broad curriculum is not an outdated idea. This approach is advocated in the National Curriculum of England: for Key Stages 1 and 2 (children aged 5 to 7 and 7 to 11 years respectively), there are well over 50 references to links with other subjects, and almost as many examples of links with ICT alone. All this is in addition to two pages that promote curriculum-wide use of language and ICT. This means that teachers have at least an 'official' precedent to plan and execute a well thought-out cross-curricular approach to their teaching. Further, as the authors have discovered in their visits to schools, there are teachers who are convinced that at least some cross-curricular teaching is certainly desirable. The National Curriculum gives examples of how this can be done, and we shall elaborate upon these where relevant throughout the book. A natural emphasis will be on those that show how ICT should be used in the teaching of the Foundation Subjects, and alongside these we give many tried and tested ideas of our own.

The proper use of the computer can be an invaluable asset in any subject, even those that at first sight may seem to have no need of it. Art is perhaps one such example, and we will have more to say about this later. However, when teaching any subject, it is at what stage in the proceedings to include ICT and how to do this that is all important. For example, there are good 'art' programs that allow children to produce coloured pictures, and while these will certainly not be great art, the programs are a very valuable tool to help motivate children both in art and in ICT itself. However, when looking at natural colours, i.e. those colours that make up white light, most textbooks and computer programs that the authors have seen show the seven distinct colours of the rainbow, whereas if we show these colours in the classroom using a prism, or even just a plastic ruler, it is very unlikely that anyone could pick out seven individual colours with the naked eye. To do this you would probably require a special instrument that measures wavelengths. It is even questionable what Newton himself made of it! Better to ask the children what they see, and then base the subsequent practical investigations, whether it be art or science, on their observations. It is at this stage that good, relevant ICT will be invaluable, for it may well help to explain this apparent anomaly. But remember, there is often great benefit in allowing children to experiment first, without the use of technology.

The role of the teacher

The authors are keen to make it clear that we are not suggesting for one moment that the computer should take the place of a good teacher! It may, to some extent, for distance learning with adults: but there are too many obvious reasons why this should not happen in schools. Indeed, we do not think ICT should even replace the practical, 'hands-on' element of learning within so many individual subjects in the primary curriculum. It is this kind of work that is so important to children, both to motivate their learning and to help them fully understand the processes and concepts involved. For this reason alone, this book is not just a quick guide for using computers in the classroom. We do include many suggestions about how all aspects of ICT hardware and software can be used, and where necessary give detailed instructions. However, it is when and how the agreed programs are used within the individual subject that is of paramount importance.

Although science is not one of the subjects in this book, it does nevertheless provide many examples of the right and wrong way to use ICT. The authors were recently viewing one of many CD-Roms that show work on electrical circuits. Not only was the level of the work below the standard we would expect older primary school children to attain, we felt that by only using this program they would never have really understood what circuits were all about anyway! Much better to give them wire, batteries and bulbs and, with a little guidance, let them find out for themselves how they work. The CD-Rom could then have been used to reinforce their understanding. Better still, they could construct a database or spreadsheet to list and record their discoveries about, for example, the electrical conductivity of the materials they used.

A broad curriculum

As teachers, we all have a duty to see that our pupils can read and write, and are taught to become as numerate as their age and ability allow. The authors have had something to say about this in their previous books. However, it does seem to us that all the recent 'initiatives' – arising from an increasingly centralized bureaucracy – have left teachers with little room for curriculum development within the school. Moreover, the emphasis on the 'basics' seems to be very 'Victorian'. Even the suggestion that classroom assistants should take on more teaching is reminiscent of the old monitor system. While we can see how this came about when mass education was first introduced, it was relatively soon recognized as being an undesirable method of education for just the reasons that we have discussed – it produced a very narrow curriculum.

By the beginning of the last century, various organizations began to appear, such as the School Natural Science Society, set up for the specific purpose of helping to provide a more interesting and challenging curriculum. In this instance it was for children in primary schools, for it was realized even then that young children could cope with advanced concepts, as long as these were introduced to them in a sensible and thoughtful way. It was also understood that the suggestion 'that they should wait until they are older' – or as some would have it today, 'that children can do all that in the secondary school' – simply ignored all that we know about child development. Are we going to have to begin this cycle again?

Our children need to understand their own environment, as well as the wider world, with all its problems, pressures and opportunities. They also need to understand something of the society in which they live, and their place within it. In short, if we want to give them a chance of becoming thinking and caring adults, who have not, at an early age, been turned away from learning, then we must offer them a richer education than just the 'three Rs' – however 'modern' the teaching of them might be.

These arguments are not new. Not so long ago, some universities insisted that science graduates should attend special lectures to *broaden their minds* (our italics). Peter Medawar, in his book *The Limits of Science*, decried this as being an insult to all concerned. He was obviously quite right to disapprove, for as he later says,

A young scientist who has not the initiative to read books, listen to music, or visit art galleries, and argue about cultural likes and dislikes, is in a plight that cannot be remedied. . .

The authors recognize that not every child will automatically reflect a wider curriculum and become a 'well-rounded personality'. However, they should be given the chance. We wonder how the situation described above came about; and in this instance, if it could not be remedied, like any such problem we should perhaps look for the cause. We can at least suggest that in part, it might have been both the result of specializing at too early an age, and by a too limited curriculum. Young children have the capacity to be interested in a wide range of subjects, activities and interests, and in many cases they are eager to learn. Waiting until a later stage in their school careers, however more sophisticated the teaching approach, will often be too late. When they face examinations and other social pressures, a broad range of subjects is not always possible. We need to have given children insights into many subjects before this stage. As we have already said, by placing administrative pressures on both teachers and young pupils, which results in a narrowing of the curriculum, we are bound to reproduce the situation that Medawar described.

One of the first attempts to highlight the dangers of the narrowing curriculum was the report *All Our Futures: Creativity, Culture and Education*, published in 1999 produced by a group of prominent names in the fields of the Arts, Letters, Business and Entertainment, under the chairmanship of Professor Ken Robinson. It suggested to the then Secretary of State for Education that there was too much formative testing and that undue emphasis on the core subjects alone would be detrimental to the curriculum as a whole. Not a lot has been heard of this report since, but perhaps it may have been taken down and dusted off to help produce the recent Primary Strategy!

One difficulty often put forward for teaching a wide variety of subjects is the amount of time available. Certainly with all the written preparation, recording, planning, testing, together with the demands of the 'core subjects', teachers certainly have a sound case to make. However, time has always been a problem. When it was first suggested that science should be taught in all primary schools, lack of time was always an argument against its introduction. In the early 1970s when the first primary science schemes were produced, not many schools seemed to take them seriously. This was of course long before the National Curriculum, literacy and numeracy hours and even direct government intervention. Perhaps it was the inflexibility shown by some teachers at that time towards a wider curriculum that partly led to the literacy and numeracy hours being introduced – inflexibility made legal!

Accepting that the proper use of ICT can give teachers more time for other subjects, if we want to teach a broader curriculum then we may still need to re-think the school week. In our previous books, as well as in our other writings (see Bibliography on page 9), we have asked if the literacy and numeracy hours need be taught every day. If they were taught on only three or perhaps four days, there would be more time for other subjects.

Perhaps a 'three day week' would even increase productivity in literacy and numeracy, for has there not been a precedent for three-day weeks increasing industrial productivity?

ICT and a 'child-centred' approach to teaching

The authors trust that this book will show how ICT can give many opportunities for individual learning. Recently, one of the authors was shown a 'training' video recording of a classroom lesson in a primary school. The video was part of the standard introduction to the Primary Strategy, and purported to show a new approach to primary teaching. What it actually showed of course was a style of teaching well known to both authors, and to most of the audience watching the video who were in the main lecturers (many of them until recently classroom teachers). It is what is known as child-centred education.

Even before the Plowden Report (1967), this form of teaching had been far from unusual. At its best, it meant that the curriculum was tailored to the needs of the child, and not a rigid framework forced upon every child irrespective of their strengths and weaknesses, natural aptitudes, learning styles or levels of attainment. To some extent this approach is being reinvented, as is shown by that Primary Strategy training video, and indeed in some secondary schools, where it is called 'Personalised Learning'. However, it should be understood that the latter is often not so much a style of teaching, but rather a statistical method of calculating levels of attainment and target-setting.

Since the advent in England of the National Curriculum, and even more so the National Literacy and Numeracy Strategies, child-centred education seems to have taken a back seat. The pressures placed upon teachers by these, together with standardised assessment tasks (SATs) and the necessity to record pupil results and achievement in ever-increasing detail, seem to have led inevitably in some cases to a change of teaching style, as well as a narrowing of the curriculum – despite the national requirement for it to be 'Broad and Balanced'. This is not the case in all schools, of course. The authors have visited many where a wide curriculum is taught in an imaginative and interesting way. Their curriculum may include literacy and numeracy hours, together with the SATS and the keeping of good and relevant records, but it will also allow for the teaching of all the so-called Foundation Subjects. It may even include one or two more!

ICT, differentiation and planning

The term 'mixed ability teaching' seems to have gone out of fashion, although differentiation, which surely amounts to much the same thing, is a required part of any good planning. Mixed ability teaching often meant that children not only studied at their own pace, but also studied varied and different aspects of the same subject. The introduction of the term 'differentiation' seemed to mark a shift from this towards a more careful and structured approach to help children with any particular difficulties that they might have with learning. Differentiation should nevertheless remain 'child centred', and with ICT included in all areas of the curriculum, this will inevitably involve the use of the computer by both the teacher and the pupil. This will eliminate much duplication in the planning process, so helping the teacher.

In the case of the child, the authors have often discovered that when given the opportunity to work with a computer, many children who seem to have difficulties in certain areas, i.e. literacy, writing, or basic numeracy, soon become as competent as their peers. Perhaps the differences were more apparent then real, but it took the computer to sort them out! Indeed, the findings of the *ImpaCT2* research project proved that pupils who were in schools that were significant users of ICT did better in a range of subjects right across the curriculum than those pupils who were not. Therefore, if we were to introduce a little of the old-fashioned mixed ability approach into our planning, we would also find more time for teaching other subjects.

In this book the authors attempt to show how we might do this, and although various subjects may have their own chapters, we do not mean this to exclude the possibilities for cross-curricular work. Indeed, we make no apologies for highlighting them at every opportunity. We give subjects their own chapters for the sake of clarity, simplicity and structure. In this way we can make it clear to the reader where the linkages and points of overlap between subjects occur, without making the whole system too complex. We have no wish to hide the wood for the trees!

We will round off this introduction with an example of a potential cross-curricular topic.

Box 0.1 The difference ICT can make

Some years ago, one of the authors visited a school when a Year 6 class was making a study of animals in special environments. This was an interesting idea, for it included aspects of both geography and science, although it was not clear at the time which of these subjects, if either, was being taught. Unfortunately, resources were limited; rather surprising in this school, although it was before computers became a regular sight in all primary classrooms. The children were copying details about the animals from general knowledge books, cutting their written work out and pasting it into various 'topic-books'.

No doubt some of them enjoyed the work, although perhaps a half-hour or so in the library might have done just as well (of course, they would then have had nothing concrete to show for their time, unless of course you could count what was in their heads!).

Using ICT in this topic

Let us think how this topic could be enhanced if computers had been part of their learning. One group was studying penguins. It is an interesting bird in many ways. One of its more obvious characteristics is that it does not fly. This provides an important teaching point, and one that could give the teacher a chance to ask some interesting questions. The authors are sure that teachers today would not ignore this opportunity, although sadly at the time none of the children despite their writing had noticed it. Today, the proper use of the computer would allow them to discover much more about this bird. Although it cannot fly, this is not a handicap as it lives in a specialized environment, where flight is unnecessary; or at least was until man came along. However, it can swim like a fish, which is of course its main food. A study such as this can lead on to so many things. How many other flightless birds are there, and what is so special about their environments? Where are they found? (Children will find that most of these birds seem to live only in the southern hemisphere – the ostrich may be the exception – which can pose some difficult but very interesting questions.) Computers can help the children discover the answers to these questions, as well as providing much background information. Computers can link them to zoos via the web, and produce and print maps, charts and data. They can also provide historical and literary references at a touch of a button. In short, they can turn what was a somewhat limited exercise into an exciting and interesting project, involving geography, science, perhaps history and mathematics, and of course the good use of language – all linked together by the imaginative use of ICT.

The boxed case studies included in this book illustrate how teachers and students are in fact carrying out just this kind of project, and we will give other similar examples. We will suggest how databases and spreadsheets can be used to collate evidence, or just to make the gathering of data more relevant and interesting; how these can also be used in a variety of subjects such as geography or even history, together with other areas of computer technology such as data logging; and the value of using a good, user-friendly CD-Rom. While it can almost be taken for granted that computers should be an integral part of any technological subject, their use can bring a new dimension to subjects like PE, art, music and modern languages. As we have stated earlier, we do not wish to imply that the computer is omnipotent. When teaching art or music it will not produce a great painting or write a symphony. It will not take the place of a brush or paint, voice or musical instrument. Nevertheless, in this book we will suggest ways in which children's learning in these subjects can be enhanced, and they in turn motivated by the proper use of computers and suitable associated hardware and software.

All children can benefit from the imaginative use of the computer in whatever subject is being taught. It should never be used as a special prize for those children who 'finish first'. We suggested earlier in this introduction that for many children who have special learning difficulties, using computers together with the appropriate software can help them to overcome at least some of their problems. While this book is written for teachers of all primary age children, if the teaching is to be in any way 'child centred', then it is necessary for us to take into account any special area of software that will help particular children. We have tried to do this where relevant, just as we have highlighted some hardware, such as the interactive whiteboard, which will be of special value to the teacher. We have naturally used and identified references where necessary, but we admit that much of what we have written derives from our own experiences. While taking responsibility for what we have written, we trust that the content reflects a balanced, unbiased, and of course helpful aspect of modern primary education.

Including ICT in all subject planning

At this point, the authors would like to make it clear that we do think that good, relevant planning is very important. We have already made references to it, and do so throughout the book. Indeed, our first chapter is about the planning and preparation, not only for individual lessons, but also for longer projects, as well as long-term planning in general, and of course the importance of including good ICT. How else could all these subjects be incorporated into a school's curriculum without careful thought and planning? We also suggest ways in which both literacy and numeracy can benefit from links with these subjects, as well as with ICT. They all require good written work, clear descriptions, and unambiguous instructions. Others, such as geography, contain a considerable amount of mathematics and science. Children will benefit if all these subjects can be included in the wider curriculum through intelligent and imaginative planning.

We started this introduction with a quotation from Edward de Bono's book, *Children Solve Problems*. It was first published in 1972, long before computers found their way into primary schools. In the book he argues the case for encouraging and indeed teaching children to think. At that time he felt that the only two areas where thinking was actively encouraged were in business and in the developing world of the computer. Whatever we may now believe of the former, computers at least are now part of school life, as are also, one hopes, the other aspects of logical and lateral thinking that he describes. It is a book that has been read by many people interested in education, and should be prescribed reading for all education administrators, and those responsible for the writing of any lesson plan, syllabus or national curriculum.

Bibliography

Bono, E. De (1972) *Children Solve Problems*. Penguin Education, London.

DES (1967) *Children and their Primary Schools* (Plowden Report). London, HMSO.

DES (1999) *The National Curriculum for England*. DfES/QCA, London.

DfEE (1999) *All Our Futures: Creativity, Culture, and Education*. HMSO, London.

DfES (2003) *Excellence and Enjoyment: A Strategy for Primary Schools*. DfES, London.

Ennever, L., et al. (1972) *With Objectives in Mind: A Guide to Science 5–13*. Macdonald Educational, London.

Medawar, P. (1984) *The Limits of Science*. Oxford University Press, Oxford.

Williams, J. and Easingwood, N. (2003) *ICT and Primary Science*. RoutledgeFalmer, London.

Williams, J. and Easingwood, N. (2004) *ICT and Primary Mathematics – A Teacher's Guide*. RoutledgeFalmer, London.

Williams, J. and Easingwood, N. (2006) *Teaching and Learning Primary Science with ICT.* Ed. P. Warwick, E. Wilson and M. Winterbottom. Chapters 3 and 9. Open University Press, Buckinghamshire.

Useful websites

For readers wishing to find out more about the Primary Strategy, they should visit the DfES website – www.standards.dfes.gov.uk/primary

For those interested in the ImpaCT2 Research Project, they should visit any Becta website.

Planning, Preparing and Delivering the Lesson

1

The role of ICT

Incorporating ICT into any lesson is one of the most difficult aspects of primary teaching. This is because the teacher has to effectively teach two subjects simultaneously: the subject element for that lesson, and also the appropriate ICT component. Furthermore, ICT often holds two key roles within the Curriculum. It has the status of a discrete subject in its own right, which usually means that pupils have a legal entitlement for access to an ICT-specific curriculum; and pupils are also encouraged to have access to ICT to support their learning in most other subjects. As a consequence, it is very important that the teacher is clear about which role ICT is playing during any particular lesson – is it a discrete ICT lesson, where ICT is being taught explicitly, or (for example) a history lesson where ICT is being used to support the delivery of the historical content? This will directly impact upon the teaching and learning objectives for that lesson and, in particular, whether they are taken from the ICT or history curriculum.

The ideal solution both educationally and organizationally is to try to deliver both the subject and ICT components together. There are two good reasons for this. First, from a purely pragmatic viewpoint, there is insufficient time in most primary school timetables to ensure sufficient coverage of all subjects (of which there are ten in the UK) in any great depth, so if two or more subjects can be delivered together then inevitably time will be saved. This cross-curricular approach is a traditional strength of the primary education system in the UK anyway, and one which the National Primary Strategy (www.standards.dfes.gov.uk/primary) advocates; so there are clear advantages for taking this approach. Furthermore, children learn in a cross-curricular way; they do not learn skills, values or attitudes in isolation, so they should find it easier to learn in this manner, and with careful and detailed planning this can be achieved relatively easily. Second, and perhaps most importantly, a curriculum for ICT is generally concerned with developing ICT capability – the knowledge, skills and understanding of when, when not and how to use ICT effectively, rather than just being relegated to a set of isolated, meaningless key skills. ICT capability is most effectively developed when it is placed firmly in the context of another subject, for then any key skills that are taught will have relevance and meaning, along with an understanding of why ICT is being used in this particular context. This is helpful to the teacher, as it ensures that ICT can legitimately be used to support other areas of the Curriculum while still being delivered as a discrete subject in its own right.

A valuable source of information for teachers is the National Curriculum website, which can be accessed at www.nc.uk.net, together with its associated website National Curriculum in Action, which can be accessed at www.ncaction.org.uk. Both sites provide plenty of helpful advice on how ICT can be incorporated into every other subject in the curriculum. The National Curriculum in Action site is particularly helpful, as for each subject area it specifically mentions ICT learning, ICT statutory requirements, ICT Opportunities, and Hardware and Software. Even for those parts of the world that do not follow this particular curriculum, these are useful sources of information.

Why use ICT?

Given that the teacher is effectively teaching two subjects simultaneously, including the use of resources that might be unfamiliar (such as laptops, palmtops, digital cameras, scanners and specialist subject software), in an environment that might be removed from the teacher's usual classroom (e.g. an ICT suite, outdoors, or another place altogether, such as a museum), then it might be tempting to ask: why it is worth going to all the bother of using ICT at all? All of the Curriculum subjects have been taught effectively and imaginatively in primary schools for many years without computers, with some superb work resulting, while the widespread availability of computers has occurred relatively recently. Yet the impact that computers can have on all aspects of the primary curriculum is proving to be profound. The effective use of ICT can truly enhance the delivery of all subjects. It can bring to subjects such as History or Geography, PE or Design and Technology, whole new aspects of learning, which were unimaginable even ten years ago. The extensive use of art packages to support Art and Design, digital video editing software to support PE and Games, control technology hardware and software to support Design and Technology, and the use of Internet and email has provided opportunities for teachers and their pupils that 20 years ago might have belonged in the realms of science fiction. It is these value-added factors, the aspects of new learning and teaching that simply would not be possible without the use of ICT, which make the place and purpose of ICT within the Foundation Subjects fundamentally important. Above all, it is the fact that it is the pupils who are using the technology in an interactive way which has provided the biggest impact on teaching and learning. The teacher needs to try and utilize this aspect of learning, and capitalize upon it. This need not be difficult, but it is different and to a certain extent a 'leap of faith' is required by the teacher. However, once this has been done, the results can be spectacular indeed!

Key points to consider when planning for ICT use

When planning the lesson, it is important to remember that in order for the full potential of the computer to be harnessed, it should be the pupil who is in control of the technology, rather than the teacher or the program on the computer. The teacher needs to plan and prepare for this, in light of the fact that pupils will have different learning styles (in that they will be principally kinaesthetic, auditory or visual learners). ICT is an excellent vehicle for supporting pupils with these different learning styles. *High Standards, High Status (Circular 4/98)* identified and introduced four key advantages that ICT brings to teaching and learning, which underpinned Initial Teacher Training in England from 1999 to 2002, as well as the New Opportunities funded ICT training programme for serving teachers. Although the document itself has now been superseded, the four key areas remain an important checklist when considering the advantages that ICT can bring to primary education. These are:

- Interactivity
- Provisionality
- Capacity and range
- Speed and automatic function

These four aspects provide the pedagogical basis upon which the lesson should be based, and are explained in greater depth below.

Interactivity

Interactivity is the most fundamentally important aspect of using ICT with children. Pupils should interact with the computer and be in control of the technology, using it as a tool to further their own learning and enquiry rather than the computer being in control of the child. It is critical that they are not passive recipients of whatever is displayed on the screen, just sitting and watching video clips or providing simple, closed answers to a series of simple, closed questions. Therefore, teachers need to think very carefully before giving pupils access to software such as drill and practice programs, although these types tend rather to be produced for literacy and numeracy practice and reinforcement rather than for the Foundation Subjects – and we might even question their value for those two subjects. Nonetheless, it is likely that CD-Roms and the Internet will be used for teaching subjects such as History and Geography, so the teacher needs to ensure that the pupils are actively engaged and are interacting with the programs concerned. Although some of this material is very good, much of it is not, and care needs to be taken when selecting this type of media for use in the lesson. It is always preferable to use an application program such as Microsoft Word, Publisher or PowerPoint, where the pupils are clearly in control of both the hardware and software, such as when they are creating original material using a word processor, desk-top publishing package or presentation software; or when integrating graphics and digital images produced by a scanner or a still or video camera into their work. Examples of open-ended work include capturing and editing digital video films, designing their own websites and using LOGO and control technology. Here the children are effectively programming the computer and using it as a means to be genuinely creative – and thus it is acting as a powerful learning tool.

However, interactivity doesn't end with using the hardware and software. As an integral part of the teaching and learning process, the teacher also needs to be interactive, actively engaging with both the pupils and the computer. For all their power and potential, computers are only as good as the use to which they are put and the data that is put into them. When used as open-ended tools by young children, the teacher's input is needed more than ever to ensure that computers are appropriately used and that the pupils are actively engaged. Despite what was said in some quarters 20 or so years ago about computers replacing teachers, this has not, and will not, happen! As with all areas of the curriculum, effective learning as well as the effective use of ICT by the pupil demands good teaching – the pupils need to be taught how to use the software and guided to use it in an appropriate manner, and then helped through the task to reach a logical and meaningful conclusion. If the teacher does not do this, then in most cases effective learning will not take place. Although some free exploration is a good thing when pupils are introduced to new hardware and software, in order to find out how software works and what it does, the best learning can not all take place simply by osmosis, and because of pressures of time, the children need to be guided and steered in the right direction.

This effective teaching involves setting challenging activities that are appropriate for all ages and abilities within the class, introducing them clearly and confidently to the pupils, and then ensuring that this focus is maintained while the pupils are actively engaged with the technology. This means asking focused, yet sufficiently open-ended questions that are designed to extend children's learning as they work. This is a powerful element in the teaching and learning process and, as such, should not be underestimated. Questions of the 'what would happen if . . . ?' or 'What happens when . . . ?' type will extend pupils' thinking skills and can significantly increase learning within the lesson.

Provisionality

All information that is produced and subsequently stored electronically on digital media is provisional. This means that nothing produced on a computer is ever entirely permanent. Work can be produced and subsequently improved, refined or edited at any point in the future – the same day, the following day, the following week or even five years later. This information can also be moved electronically around the world via email or file transfer protocol (FTP – for moving huge files, particularly useful for posting on the World Wide Web), or can be saved onto a disk, CD-Rom, external hard drive or camera and physically transported elsewhere. It is this constant ability to edit and refine that is powerful – any piece of work can be updated without leaving any trace whatsoever of possibly a dozen or more changes that it may have gone through. This is particularly useful for the more reluctant pupil, especially in writing-based tasks, as there will be no crossings or rubbing out – a perfect copy will be produced every time, so the pupil will not become demoralized. By updating and saving with a new file name, the teacher will be able to track any changes that the pupils have made in their work for assessment purposes.

Box 1.1   A writing activity

Additionally, files can be copied and subsequently used in a number of different ways. For example, a group of children might write a story collaboratively as part of their studies in History, RE or Citizenship. This can be done by involving one computer, several computers, a whole room of computers or even the Internet and email. In an ICT suite, the children can sit in pairs at a computer and begin a story. After a few minutes, the teacher suddenly stops the children working and moves each pair onto a different machine. They then continue the story in front of them; and this is repeated several times until the story is finished, not unlike the old party game of consequences. (It is important though to let the children move to another computer randomly, otherwise this activity does not work as well, as following the same pupils tends to give similar responses).

Alternatively, pairs of children can write the story on one computer, writing a paragraph each (or for younger children perhaps the line of a poem) until it is finished. The work can be saved at every step of the way for assessment purposes by the teacher, and it can then be finished off by the addition of images, clip art, borders and different sizes, styles and colours of font. The work can then be saved and emailed to another school anywhere in the

English-speaking world for further comment and development. None of this would be possible without a computer, and the work can evolve in many different ways, often involving dozens of pupils in several countries.

Box 1.2 A visual activity

A similar yet interesting development of the last activity involves the making of a film using a digital video camera. Small groups of children could make a short film and then download the resulting unedited footage onto the computer. Using a simple video editing tool such as Windows Movie Maker, the film can then be edited in many different ways – in much the same way that text is edited – to give a different resulting final film, all from the same 'raw' footage. This can include editing out unwanted scenes, copying and pasting in extra ones, and adding titles and transitions between scenes, background music or voice-overs and special effects. In this example the children are being creative twice – once during the original filming, and again during the editing. The film is only 'finished' when it is rendered and saved as a film in the desired format, and again, the original footage can still be saved on the original camera tape or on the computer in its unedited form. (We explain how to do this in greater detail in Chapter 8.)

Capacity and range

One of the main advantages of computers is that they can handle huge amounts of different types of data and/or information individually or simultaneously. The fact that one computer can be used for so many completely different things is an extremely powerful tool; as far as the primary classroom is concerned, these normally include:

- word processing – for writing documents which can incorporate a range of images and clip art
- desk top publishing (DTP) – for producing newsletters, posters, cards etc.
- database – for organizing and managing information
- spreadsheet – for manipulating numbers
- control – for controlling external objects, e.g. traffic lights, automated features
- data logging – for collecting environmental data and presenting it as information
- graphics – for producing pictures.

In addition to these different types of application, the computer can also act as a driver for:

- CD-Roms and other educational multimedia
- Internet browser – for searching the World Wide Web
- email – for communications around the world via computer
- digital still and video camera – for producing still and video images
- scanners – to enable documents and pictures to be scanned into a computer for subsequent use within other programs

- printers – to allow any work that is produced to be printed out
- interactive whiteboards – to enable both pupils and teachers to demonstrate ideas to the other members of the class.

Speed and automatic function

As can be seen from the list above, computers can handle large amounts of different kinds of data and information and can perform many different, powerful functions. However, the real advantage of the computer is that it does all of these things quickly, automatically and often simultaneously. For example, when producing a newsletter in Microsoft Publisher, the children can insert images which are collected via a scanner or digital camera, or even from the World Wide Web (assuming copyright clearance has been obtained). Text can be inserted from a range of other sources. This power means that the computer can be used to remove the manual element from pupils' work, for example colouring the bars on a histogram, so they can spend time accessing higher levels of intellectual engagement and understanding, hypothesizing and analysing their findings and drawing sensible and meaningful conclusions rather than becoming bogged down with laborious pedantic tasks.

This in turn will have a great motivating effect on pupils. Children love using this sort of technology, and are very motivated not only *to* use it, but also when they *are* using it. This is very important and the effects should not be underestimated. Motivating children is the essential ingredient for them to become effective learners, and the use of ICT helps greatly with this. However, using ICT should not be an end in itself, for not only will that undermine exactly what we have described above, but could also potentially demotivate pupils, as simple repetitive tasks even on the computer are boring. This is not the case if ICT is used in connection with work from another subject. Most children have ready access to technology at home – often hardware and software that is as good as, or even better than that which they use in school. As a consequence of this, it is important to ensure that pupils receive an education involving ICT that is interesting and original. This is why it is crucially important that teaching be active, learning be interactive and that the pupil is completely in control of the technology – not the other way round.

Collaboration

Another advantage of using ICT is that it acts as a very effective focal point for collaborative work. This is particularly important in the primary school, where the development of personal and social skills is traditionally seen as being as important as the more academic aspects of school life. The computer can act as a conduit for learning, perhaps through the use of a digital camera or a scanner. A group can then collaborate to produce a piece of work on the computer. It is important to remember that collaborative work is an educational device, not an organizational one. If one or more members of the group are for any reason withdrawn, then the whole dynamics of the group and the activity will be fundamentally changed, and the collaborative nature of the task will be irrevocably altered. When a group is arranged on an organizational basis this will not happen – this might occur when a group of pupils are working on a similar activity but on an individual basis. The teacher needs to be clear exactly what sort of grouping is taking place when planning the lesson.

When planning the lesson, the teacher needs to remember these key advantages of using ICT and use these as part of the pedagogical rationale for the lesson – that is, why ICT is being used, and how it is going to be taught and learnt from an educational perspective. If one or all of these advantages are not utilized then there is little point in using the technology. It is a waste of a valuable resource which could be better used elsewhere. In the normal course of events, there is little point in using several thousand pounds' worth of ICT hardware and software on a task that could just as easily be achieved using pencil and paper methods. The use of ICT must provide a value added component – that is, it must add something to the lesson that would simply be impossible otherwise. Once this is appreciated, good lessons that are based upon an effective educational pedagogy will inevitably result.

Units of study

The next challenge is to identify appropriate opportunities to use this power to enhance teaching and learning in the Foundation Subjects, and to decide how ICT will be used.

Most of the Foundation Subjects of the National Curriculum for England are arranged into units of study. These are often delivered to primary classes in half-term blocks, so in theory approximately six units of each subject can be delivered during the course of a school year. However, due to time constraints, largely determined by the emphasis placed upon the core subjects of English, Mathematics and Science, there is no requirement for all of the Foundation Subjects to be taught at any one time. Therefore, there may be a situation in a particular class where Art and Geography are being taught in a given half-term period, but History and Design and Technology are not. This does not matter; curriculum coverage should balance out over the course of the school year.

Once the decision has been made to use ICT to support the delivery of a particular aspect of a Foundation Subject, the teacher needs to make some important decisions about the extent to which ICT is to be employed, and what role it is to take. We have already seen that ICT can take two distinct roles in a lesson: either as a discrete subject, or as a support to the teaching and learning of other subjects. Given that this book is about ICT supporting the Foundation Subjects, this will be the prime focus that this discussion will take; but it is also important to remember that there is a section in the National Curriculum for ICT in England, which suggests that ICT can be taught as a subject on its own. Some QCA Schemes of Work for ICT also suggest this to be the case. However, as we have made clear above, ICT is at its best when used in support of other subjects, even when occasionally the emphasis of the lesson rests on the use of the computer alone. For example, the 'Communicating and Handling Information' strand will be used many times over in the delivery of the Foundation Subjects in a variety of ways – continuous prose in Microsoft Word, newspapers, posters and newsletters in Microsoft Publisher and presentations in Microsoft PowerPoint.

The next step is to decide the extent to which ICT is to be used to support a unit of work. Again, the appropriateness of ICT as detailed above will be the main determining factor in this decision.

Example: Constructing a website

The use of ICT might form an integral part of an entire unit, for example a Year 5 or 6 project to construct a website concerned with the school and its immediate environment, drawing on history, geography and environmental science. In order to do this the children would need to research the history of their local area, perhaps using the Internet as a means for research. They may scan old photographs into the computer for subsequent use on the website, capture their own images with a digital camera, film video clips, or record interviews with local people that can be downloaded. This kind of primary, first-hand research is important to all subjects, as well as developing a wide range of important ICT key skills. Children would need to plan out exactly what they wanted to go on each page and also to structure the website so that it could be navigated easily. Then pupils would actually construct the site, perhaps as a collaborative learning task, with several pupils working on a particular aspect of local life to produce one page. The more able pupils could perhaps produce template pages for other members of the class to use. These would then be hyperlinked together and uploaded to a server so that they could be viewed over the Internet. This is an excellent means of developing ICT capability through a whole class project that could lead on to many future areas of study in History or Geography.

Alternatively, ICT might only be used for one or two lessons: and again, this is perfectly legitimate. As we have already seen in this chapter, there is little value in using ICT purely because it is there – it must be used appropriately. For example, a digital camera might be used to capture images of Key Stage 1 children as part of a topic on 'Ourselves', which is then inserted into a piece of text about the children and what they were doing. This might only take one lesson, or even part of one lesson, but is a powerful use of ICT nonetheless because of its speed and ease of use, compared to doing it the 'old-fashioned' way with glue and handwriting! Or, as detailed in the lesson plan in the case study below, ICT can be used for two lessons within a wider topic, but for a specific purpose. It is also important to remember that ICT includes the preparation of data and information before entering it into a computer: it is not only 'hands-on' time.

Planning the lesson

Bearing all of the above in mind, when planning a lesson where ICT is to be used the teacher will find it useful to consider the following points, in order to make the lesson effective and to increase the likelihood of making it a success.

Health and safety

First and most importantly, what health and safety aspects need to be considered? Is there light shining on the screen? Are the chairs the correct height? Are there any trailing cables? Can everybody sit at a workstation comfortably? Has a risk assessment been completed? If not, one should be as a matter of urgency. The Becta website provides additional advice here (www.becta.org.uk).

Resources

What hardware and software resources are available and how are they distributed throughout the school? This audit should include the types of computers, whether they are desktop or laptop PCs, the use of a wireless or cable network, what software is available on which computers, and where they are located. For example, is there a core provision of desktop computers in a central ICT suite, or are they dispersed around the school? Is there provision for both? Are they networked, and if so, how? If there are any laptops, are they on a trolley so that they can easily be moved and recharged for later use? Indeed, are they charged up and ready for immediate use anyway? What is the range of the wireless network? Can the computers be used outside? Do they all have the same software? Is the software suitable for effective delivery of the lesson (this is discussed in greater depth below)? Do all of the computers have the same operating system (e.g. Windows XP)? This can lead to compatibility problems if they do not. Are any Foundation Subject-specific resources needed (these might include books, pictures or artefacts)?

Software

Which software package will be used to deliver the lesson? Is it the most appropriate in order to deliver the teaching and learning objectives of the lesson? Will it provide the 'value-added' factors that the use of ICT demands? Is it sufficiently open-ended to allow the children to be in control of the software, rather than the software controlling the children, demanding simple responses? Does it actually do what you want it to do? Is it easy to use? Is it intuitive – that is, is it easy for the teacher to demonstrate or easy for the children to work out how to use themselves, or does it need a large and unwieldy manual to explain all of its functions? Does it have easy-to-follow on-screen help guides? Is it easy to navigate? Is the interface bright, clear and uncluttered? Are the graphics high quality? Are buttons large enough for young children to easily point and click with the mouse? Is it interactive? Does it allow the user to take the initiative, or does the user have to follow instructions closely to make it work? Is there an options facility, so the teacher can change the settings and levels of difficulty? And are these hidden, so that younger children cannot inadvertently access them and change the settings themselves?

Teaching and learning objectives

What are the teaching and learning objectives of the lesson (for this example we are assuming that this is a Foundation Subject where ICT is being used to support the teaching and learning)? Where have these objectives come from? The National Curriculum? The QCA Schemes of Work? The school's own planning or curriculum? This lesson has to come from somewhere – for the sake of continuity and progression and appropriateness to a particular age and ability of children, there needs to be a source. This will usually be the school's own medium-term planning, which in turn may be drawn from the National Curriculum for England and the QCA Schemes of Work. These are available online at www.standards.dfes.gov.uk/schemes.

The purpose of ICT

The teacher will need to decide for what purposes ICT is being used (this will of course be in the context of the subject that is being taught). Is it for assessing learning, reinforcing a skill, learning new material or extending previous learning? As a consequence, will the software be a didactic program, such as a drill and practice program, or be concerned with problem-solving, where the pupil needs to make some decisions in order to progress through the program? This could be a simulation of an historical setting, or an application where the software acts as a tool to pupil learning, such as Microsoft Office, or even open-ended software, where the child effectively programs the computer itself. This would include aspects of ICT such as LOGO, control technology, digital video editing and web authoring.

Learning styles

How will the lesson cater for the different types of learning styles of the various pupils? How will visual, auditory and kinaesthetic learners be catered for? Will any special teaching methods be employed (for example, explaining the content to be taught in three different ways to meet the needs of each type of learner)? And as a consequence, what types of software will need to be employed?

Consistency between ICT and the relevant subject

Does the use of ICT match the level of the Foundation Subject being taught? This is an important point, and one that is all too easily overlooked. The level of ICT must match the level of the content of the subject. If the level of difficulty of the ICT that is used is higher, then this will seriously hamper the delivery of the subject content, as the use of ICT will act as a barrier to accessing what is needed to deliver the Foundation Subject component, and will negate the point of the lesson. Care needs to be taken here to ensure that the ICT components in the National Curriculum, QCA Schemes of Work and school planning directly match up with the corresponding levels of work in the equivalent documents for the Foundation Subject that is to be taught.

Classroom organization and management

How is the class to be organized and managed? Again, this will largely depend on all of the above, but the organization and the management of the lesson will depend very much on the location of the lesson, the subject primarily being taught, the objectives to be met and the equipment that is to be used. Also, the teacher needs to decide whether any additional adult help is needed for supervision and help in using the equipment – especially so with the youngest children, and when it is specialist equipment that is being used, such as digital cameras and scanners. Additional help may also be needed for those children with special educational needs and those who are working to an individual education plan.

Teaching assistants

Will additional help be available to you during the lesson? If so, how will this be deployed? Will the teaching assistant work solely with those children with special educational needs and those who are working to an individual education plan, or will they be used in a much wider role? Will they support the more able children, extending at the upper end of the ability scale? Will they work with the middle band of pupils, or perhaps those who need extra help without having an individual education plan (it is these pupils who often benefit the most from this sort of support)? Do they have good ICT skills and so are able to be used in a much broader way? Whatever happens, the teacher needs to indicate clearly what particular role the teaching assistants are to play. This can be done in writing, either with a copy of the lesson plan or a special list of tasks with the required learning outcomes.

Other adult helpers

As with teaching assistants, the teacher needs to be clear how additional help might be employed. This might concern working on a one-to-one basis with individuals, or be used for a specific task, such as working with a group using a floor turtle or a digital camera.

How the lesson is to be delivered

Will the lesson be delivered as a 'standard' three-part lesson – that is, a starter, a working phase where the children complete a task, and a plenary? Or will it be 'chunked', that is, divided up into several smaller parts with each individual idea taught and reinforced by the children immediately and separately (bearing in mind that the lesson may be a relatively small part of an on-going project)?

Developing ICT capability

How is ICT capability being developed? What knowledge, skills and understanding are being developed? How are they being taught – through another subject or as part of a discrete ICT lesson? In the former case, though the focus is primarily on a Foundation Subject, this will provide an ideal opportunity to meet the requirements of the ICT curriculum.

Differentiation

This is very difficult where ICT is used, mainly due to the fact that there are both subject and ICT components to the lesson. Some children find both difficult, whereas others will be stronger at one aspect than the other. There are also some children who will be strong at both. The teacher needs to consider this carefully. How will the lesson be differentiated? Will different tasks be set for pupils of differing abilities: for example, work set individually or perhaps at three different levels – high ability, middle ability and lower ability? The QCA Schemes of Work for ICT allow for three different ability levels, so using these might prove to be particularly helpful. Useful strategies here include worksheets at different levels, and children paired or grouped according to ability.

In the authors' experience, mixed-ability groups do not always work where ICT is involved. There are several reasons for this. Some children need the program to be highly animated, while others require this less. Some less able children often find it difficult to match the input speeds of the more able children, causing everybody to become frustrated. It might simply be the relative speed and understanding by the children of the programs themselves. Although we would not normally advocate too much emphasis on grouping by ability only, in this instance there is no definite answer to what is an ongoing issue in primary education.

Differentiated tasks and groupings by ability levels can help here. The notion of 'differentiation by outcome' is difficult – isn't this assessment? One example where mixed ability and ICT can work is when the computer is used as a word processor to write an 'old-fashioned' story. We have often seen groups of children of a wide range of abilities all working at the same computer, each having a similar input and all benefiting from others' ideas.

Pupils with Special Educational Needs and those with an individual education plan

Those children with special needs and/or those on an individual education plan need to be specifically catered for as part of the lesson. Indeed, those with an individual education plan have an additional entitlement to use ICT, so the teacher needs to decide whether or not this lesson counts as part of their extra entitlement.

Interactivity

Will the children be genuinely interacting with the computer? Will they be in control of the computer, rather than the other way round? And will they also be learning the subject component as well as the ICT? Will they be engaged throughout the lesson? How will the teacher engage with both the technology and the children? How will 'active teaching and learning' occur?

'Value-added'

Is there a 'value-added' component, in that the power of using ICT is being fully exploited, or could the lesson objectives be just as easily met without a computer? If there is a value-added component, what exactly is this? Interactivity? Provisionality? It is unlikely that at this stage there is not an extra component, for surely this basic aspect would have been considered at the very start, when a decision was made that the lesson's objectives could be better achieved this way? However it is important to decide if the capacity and range of the technology is being fully exploited. The teacher needs to be able to justify why ICT is being used.

Vocabulary and keywords

The development of subject-specific vocabulary is very important for both the Foundation Subject being taught and ICT. This way, both types of vocabulary have a context.

Assessment

How are the pupils to be assessed? Is this going to be assessment for learning or assessment of learning? Given that a computer is being used, it will probably be the former.

Delivering the lesson

Once the factors listed above have been taken into consideration and are present in the plan (of which there is an example below), the next step is the delivery of the lesson itself. At the risk of repeating what has already been said, it is necessary to consider the key aspects required to achieve a successful and interesting lesson. Although the teacher will necessarily be restricted by the school's timetable and resources, this should not affect the quality of work that can be achieved. The teacher can only employ the resources that the school possesses, but, as we have already made clear, the quality of pupil work is largely down to the teacher rather than to the quality of the resources and ICT equipment that is available. Having said that, there is clearly a need for a minimum level of technology in order for a lesson to be effectively delivered with ICT, but this technology need not necessarily be as sophisticated as one might imagine. Most work in the Foundation Subjects can be effectively supported by the use of the Microsoft Office suite of programs as a minimum requirement. The quality of the teacher should always surpass the quality of the equipment, and anyway at present most primary schools have a sufficient amount of good quality hardware and software.

The example lesson that we describe below may appear to some to be more than a little structured. We are well aware of and indeed welcome the fact that some schools have a very much less rigid structure not only to the individual lesson, but to the whole school day. Nevertheless, they produce comprehensive plans for all the work done and may even use published schemes of work, although these will often be used as 'idea sheets' rather than as rigid guides. No doubt they also participate in the literacy and numeracy programmes, and for these they will need to follow a more rigid timetable. There is one very obvious reason why a lesson of this kind needs this structure: it involves the school's computers, and these are nearly always situated in one room, which has to be timetabled for use. Hence it needs very detailed planning to make the most of the limited time available. Teachers will also be aware that this lesson is only one part of an on-going topic, and that much additional work will be carried out either in the classroom, in the school grounds or even outside the school itself.

The lesson plan

The lesson will normally be delivered in three parts. This consists of a starter, a work phase and a plenary. This follows the format established by both the literacy and numeracy strategies, so should be familiar to teachers and pupils alike. Each section of the lesson is marked by a transition, where the pupils move between the phases of the lesson; and this transition will need to be carefully managed by the teacher in order for the lesson to retain coherence.

At the very beginning of the lesson, the teaching and learning objectives should be made clear to the pupils. These should be clearly displayed so that all of the children can see them, and should be referred to at regular points in the lesson. Many primary schools now use 'WALT', 'WILF' and 'TIB' as a means of reinforcing this to their children. These are:

- WALT – meaning 'We are learning to . . .'. This is the lesson objective and signals to the children what they will be learning during the lesson.
- WILF – meaning 'What I'm looking for . . .'. This is the expected outcome from the pupils – in other words, what the teacher is looking for the children to produce.
- TIB – meaning 'This is because . . .'. This describes the purpose of the activity.

(From *Unlocking Formative Assessment: Practical Strategies for Enhancing Pupils' Learning in the Primary Classroom*, Shirley Clarke.)

The authors have seen these formulae being used very successfully with a wide range of ages right across the primary phase (and into secondary education too!). They are effective because they make clear what pupils are going to learn, what is expected from them and why they are doing it. We all perform a task better when we know why we are doing it! And from the teacher's perspective, it makes assessing the lesson that much easier.

The starter will last for 15 to 20 minutes, and may begin with a short warm-up activity. This may or may not relate to the content of the rest of the lesson, although the authors prefer something related to what was being taught in the previous lesson, usually as revision and reinforcement. Once this has been completed, the remainder of the starter can act as a point for the input of the new material to be covered during the lesson. However, if there have been previous lessons and this is just one of a sequence, then this short introduction will allow for the necessary continuity and progression. This may allow the teacher to demonstrate the use of new software and also provide for the introduction of specific subject material (as opposed to purely ICT), by asking open-ended questions with a specific subject bias. It is important that the teacher remembers to give the input in two or three different ways, in order to reinforce the main teaching points and to enable visual, auditory and kinaesthetic learners to fully participate in the lesson.

While giving this initial input, it is preferable to have the children in a position where they can look at and listen to the teacher, as well as participate in class discussion. As we have mentioned before, this topic will not all be taught in one place at one time, so it might be preferable to deliver this input in the pupils' own classroom rather than the ICT suite or any other external place. This will help the children to concentrate and focus upon the matter in hand, and will also maximize the use of time with the school's scarce resources, such as access to the ICT suite or the set of laptops. For that reason it remains a good idea to have a computer and an interactive whiteboard in the classroom, although it must be installed with the same software that the pupils will actually be using. If the input has to be given in the ICT suite, then the teacher will need to employ different classroom management strategies from those used in their usual classroom. Due to space restrictions, this will probably mean that the pupils will be seated at a computer, possibly facing away from the teacher. Although this is stating the obvious, the teacher needs to get the children to physically turn their chairs to face the front of the room. Alternatively, other strategies can include getting the pupils to switch off their monitors, while leaving the computers on. It is always a good idea to switch the computers on as the children enter the room, and perhaps log on as well, for this will save time later once the children need to use the computers.

After this introduction the pupils will normally begin the working phase of the lesson. This will probably involve some movement, which will need to be carefully managed by the teacher. Once the children start work, the teacher will circulate amongst the children, asking them questions which are designed to consolidate, reinforce and extend their learning. This approach can (as we have already mentioned) extend learning by as much as 50%. The questions need to be open-ended, yet focused, and require the children to explain what they are doing or what they have done. For example the teacher might just say to a group of children: 'That looks interesting – tell me about it.'

The children's answers can also be used as evidence for formative assessment purposes. This phase of the lesson should, where possible, last a minimum of about 30 minutes. It is very important to ensure that the pupils are given sufficient 'hands-on' time. The lesson involves ICT, so they need to be given plenty of opportunity to use it. However, it is also important not to let the lesson go to the other extreme, where it 'drifts' with very little teacher input, with the children using the computers without having a clear focus as to what they should be doing. This use of good, focused questioning together with a sensible time limit for the work required will give the children a sense of purpose, so that they remain concentrated on their work.

The plenary will conclude the lesson. This final session is very important and as such should not be overlooked or underestimated. It should summarize and reinforce the previous learning and should provide a link to the next lesson. It also provides an excellent opportunity for the pupils to share the product of their learning with the other members of the class. If the lesson has been organized as a collaborative learning activity, it might also provide an opportunity to present their findings.

The three-part lesson structure allows direct teaching, pupil interaction, reinforcement of new and previous learning, and presentation to the rest of the class. However, with younger children, or those children who find concentrating difficult, it might be beneficial for the lesson to be 'chunked'. In this case the three-part lesson is further broken down into perhaps five or six parts, or even more, where the teacher teaches one small skill or idea and the children immediately go and practise it. The teacher then delivers another key teaching point and the children go and practise it again. This enables the children to maintain focus and concentration, while skills are gradually built up. This is a particularly effective method when a new piece of software is being introduced to the children, as it allows them to keep pace with the level of the knowledge required for the subject being taught, whatever that may be.

Assessing the lesson

Assessment should be an integral part of the lesson, and included at the planning stage. This is because there needs to be an explicit link between the teaching and learning objectives for the lesson, and a means of determining the extent to which these objectives have been achieved. There is little value in planning and delivering a lesson, and then deciding to do some assessment afterwards. Effective assessment can only occur when one is a direct consequence of the other.

There are several main reasons why teachers should assess during their lessons. These are:

- To identify the pupils' achievement and to indicate where they are in their learning.
- For continuity and progression purposes – to plan the next stage in pupil learning.
- To illustrate pupil progress against national targets and league tables.

- To identify those pupils who may need 'catch-up' activities.
- To help teachers to evaluate their own teaching.

In order to do this assessment there are three principal types of assessment that the teacher will employ.

Assessment for Learning (AfL)

Also known as formative assessment, this type of assessment is used for 'gathering and interpreting evidence about how and what pupils learn; and the learners and their teachers using that evidence to decide where the students are in their learning, and where they are going and how to take the next steps' (QCA and the Assessment Reform Group, 2001). This information is used when identifying pupil strengths and weaknesses, so as to inform future planning. This assessment will take place during the completion of a task by pupils, and will feed back directly into the teaching and learning process. This is illustrated by the diagram in Figure 1.1. Assessment for Learning will take place through teacher questioning and assessing pupil dialogue, written or verbal feedback from marking, peer and self-assessment and tasks and tests for formative uses. It is concerned with improving pupil performance.

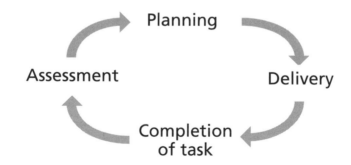

Figure 1.1 The cycle of planning, delivery and assessment. The lesson or series of lessons start with the plan. The lesson is delivered, and the children complete a task. While the lesson is in progress, the teacher carries out a range of formative assessments – this will largely concern questioning the children with open-ended, yet focused questioning. This will take the form of 'What would happen if?' types of questions, which the teacher will then record and feed back into planning for subsequent lessons.

Assessment of Learning (AoL)

Also known as summative assessment, this type of assessment is concerned with providing a grade or score as a measure or summation of learning that has taken place. A good example of this is levelling for National Curriculum or SAT purposes at the end of Key Stages 1 and 2. This will include the use of school portfolios, teacher assessments that are moderated and national tests. This type of assessment is concerned with proving pupil performance.

Diagnostic assessment

This is assessment that is used to diagnose specific problems or conditions that a pupil may appear to have. It might be in the form of a reading test to determine a child's reading age, or whether a child has any special educational needs, or indeed if they are in any way particularly gifted and talented.

The 10 principles of assessment

The QCA website for assessment details ten principles of assessment that teachers need to consider when planning, delivering and assessing lessons. These are:

1 Assessment for learning should be part of effective planning of teaching and learning.
2 Assessment for learning should focus on how students learn.
3 Assessment for learning should be recognized as central to classroom practice.
4 Assessment for learning should be regarded as a key professional skill for teachers.
5 Assessment for learning should be sensitive and constructive, because any assessment has an emotional impact.
6 Assessment for learning should take account of the importance of learner motivation.
7 Assessment for learning should promote commitment to learning goals and a shared understanding of the criteria by which they are assessed.
8 Learners should receive constructive guidance about how to improve.
9 Assessment for learning develops learners' capacity for self-assessment so that they can become reflective and self-managing.
10 Assessment for learning should recognize the full range of achievements of all learners.

Taken from the Qualifications and Curriculum Authority website at
www.qca.org.uk/ages3-14/afl/907.html (accessed April 2006).

This is an important checklist, which teachers need to consider when planning and delivering any lesson. In the light of what was written about assessment in the report *All Our Futures* (DfEE 1998/99), teachers should perhaps pay particular attention to point four.

Assessment – the problems

In order to assess any lesson where ICT is being used, the teacher needs to be completely clear on what the main focus of the lesson is. In the same way that ICT can perform two distinct functions and roles – that is as a tool for supporting a Foundation Subject, or as a discrete subject in its own right – the teacher needs to be clear about what exactly is to be assessed. If the teaching and learning objectives are focused on an aspect of a Foundation Subject, then that will be the focus of assessment. If the focus is on ICT, then that is what will be the primary focus for assessment. However, that is not to say that one cannot inform the other: if a teacher observes something concerning a pupil's ICT skills, there is no reason why that should not be recorded for future reference, be it as a formative point for development, or as a summative comment for a school report or parent's evening interview. For the purposes of this book, we will focus upon how ICT can support the Foundation Subject component.

Assessment – the solutions

In order to successfully assess pupils while they are working, there are several key things that the teacher can do. Using 'WALT', 'WILF', and 'TIB' will ensure that even the youngest pupils will be clear about what the lesson objectives are and what their role is. The assessment criteria will be clear, and both pupils and teacher will have a shared understanding of what is required in terms of outcomes from the lesson. The pupils should understand what they need to say, do or produce to achieve the objectives of the lesson, and to provide the evidence that the teacher needs when assessing or marking their work. The teacher can reinforce this by using the plenary session to reflect upon what has been accomplished, as well as in using formative assessment while the lesson is in progress. Additionally, the teacher can get more evidence for assessment by further checking pupils' understanding by using the open-ended questioning techniques. Incidentally, it is important for the teacher to allow 'wait time', that is, time to encourage the children to provide longer answers, which in turn will provide more evidence of deeper understanding, as the pupils are given time to reflect upon their learning and to explain the steps in their thinking. Additionally, it should allow more of the children time to answer the questions. The teacher also needs to consider other important aspects of the lesson, such as to what extent the pupils discussed the activity, whether or not each child had a fair part in the activity, whether any problem-solving techniques were used, and how long the children were on task.

Assessment of learning

The latter part of this chapter has concentrated on assessment for learning. This has been deliberate, as this is by far the most effective means of assessing, particularly when ICT is used. A finished piece of work, probably in the form of a print-out, will tell very little about where it came from or the many stages that it may have gone through to get to the final product. If we are to understand the complete process, there will need to be frequent involvement by both pupil and teacher. Only by observing, questioning and discussing at every stage will a teacher have the fullest appreciation of the extent to which the pupil has met the learning objectives for that lesson (or series of lessons).

From time to time, however, it will be necessary for the teacher to engage in assessment of learning – for the end of Key Stage SATs or for school reports, for instance. This will involve gathering evidence to prove the levels of attainment that have been achieved. This is difficult for several reasons. First, as we have already seen, the teacher needs to be completely clear as to what it is that is being assessed. If the ICT component is to be assessed summatively, this will usually be for levelling purposes. However, one piece of work cannot be used to provide a National Curriculum level. This is because the National Curriculum for ICT level descriptions contain elements that draw on as many as half a dozen or so different aspects of ICT. For example, the level description for level 3 ICT states that:

> Pupils use ICT to save information and to find and use appropriate stored information, following straightforward lines of enquiry. They use ICT to generate, develop, organize and present their work. They share and exchange their ideas with others. They use sequences of instructions to control devices and achieve specific outcomes. They make appropriate choices when using ICT-based models or simulations to help them find things out and solve problems. They describe their use of ICT and its use outside school.
>
> (National Curriculum Online – ICT, Attainment Target for Level 3).

Clearly, all these elements cannot be taught in one go: consequently, a level can only be awarded towards the end of each school year, when a sufficient amount of evidence has been collected. Certainly, any ICT work that the children complete will count as evidence towards the award of a level, but at least half a dozen pieces will be needed to provide this evidence.

This in turn leads to another potential difficulty – how to assign a level to a piece of work. Given that there are so many elements to each level description for ICT alone, as well as the Foundation Subject component, it is no surprise that often a teacher's assessment can be adrift by as much as two levels. Fortunately, the National Curriculum in Action website (www.ncaction.org.uk) is very helpful here. This provides exemplar work for children of a range of ages and abilities across the primary phase for all of the subjects of the National Curriculum. Like the National Curriculum Online website, it also provides a large number of explicit links detailing where ICT can be used to support all the subjects in the National Curriculum.

Box 1.3   An example of ICT being used to support the teaching of Geography

Our thanks go to Stephanie Wharton, a primary trainee teacher studying at Anglia Ruskin University in Chelmsford, for the following lesson plan and wind farm work. This was undertaken during one of her school placements with a mixed Year 5 and 6 class at Collingwood Primary School, South Woodham Ferrers, Essex.

A major local issue, which was creating much discussion and receiving a great deal of media attention, was a proposed wind farm at the nearby village of Bradwell, situated on the Essex coast. A husband of one of the school's teachers farmed in the immediate area, and as a consequence the proposal directly impacted upon them. Stephanie took the opportunity to use this as a basis for geographical investigation, as well as providing a meaningful and appropriate opportunity to use ICT with the class. Initially she completed some research herself, using the Internet to discover who the various interested parties were and what their respective points of view were – an excellent example of using ICT for professional purposes. As a result of this she was able to produce the lesson plan below, which is the first of a sequence of two lessons. As the school followed the QCA schemes of work this formed the basis for the geographical components of planning, being based on Unit 16. As can be seen, Stephanie produced an extremely detailed lesson plan covering every aspect of the topic, including learning objectives, identifying assessment opportunities, key vocabulary, resources, and differentiation, as well as detailed content and teaching points on what is to be actually taught and to whom. The more able pupils interviewed the teacher to produce a newspaper article that was presented from her perspective, while the less able pupils designed posters. A selection of these is included in Figures 1.5 to 1.7 below. To ensure that the pupils fully understood the requirements of the various tasks and that they asked the right questions, Stephanie produced two prompt sheets, and a glossary for each of the groups. These are included below as Figures 1.3 and 1.4.

In a second lesson, the children completed their newsletters and posters. During the introduction a local map was displayed so that children could find the proposed windfarm site in relation to their own village. Using the techniques of open-ended questioning, the teacher used a flipchart to record the children's answers, be they for or against the site. Much of their information had been gathered from local websites, as well as their interviews with local people (as described in the first lesson plan). The children needed a little help to understand some of the language used on the website, but all this together with the open-ended questioning proved invaluable for assessment purposes.

Figure 1.2 The first lesson plan. This contains all of the key components of a good lesson plan, including the key focus, lesson objectives, assessment opportunities, the lesson content and key teaching points, key vocabulary and resources, differentiation, content for those children with special educational needs or individual education plans, and, finally, ICT. As can be seen, there is no need to place a great emphasis on ICT, as this is fundamentally a geography lesson.

Lesson Plan

Class	Year 5/6	Date	13th May	Duration	75 mins

Focus: Geography – Unit 16: What's in the news? What is happening in our local area?	Lesson Position: 1 of 2

Learning objectives: (Where LO will be met)	Assessment opportunities
• To develop awareness of recent or proposed changes in a locality. (Intro, main lesson) • To use ICT to present information. (Lesson 2 in ICT suite)	• Through open questioning assess understanding of impact of environmental change, and that people have different views. • Focus group. • Whole class through output.

Time	Lesson content
20 mins	**Introduction:** • The main purpose of this lesson is to assess the children's prior knowledge and understanding of the proposed development from different points of view, and develop this understanding further. • This will involve using a map to illustrate the location of the proposed sites. Paying particular attention to the location in relation to homes and the school. • It will also involve sharing with the children the rationale behind such developments, looking at the environmental implications, both positive and negative. • Children will be asked in pairs to spend three minutes jotting down everything they know already about wind farms. • This will be shared and discussed and some key points in headings made on the board. • The children will then be asked in pairs to think of who might be for/against such a development. Will share and write headings on board. • Will be looking for: local residents, environmental people promoting renewable energy, wildlife people, Government. Will draw this out of children and list headings on board. • At end of introduction want to hone focus into five key areas to research: environmental; those against; local residents; impact on wildlife; existing wind farms.
45 mins	**Main lesson:** • Advise children of pairings arranged to ensure mixed-ability peer support provided. • Explain that three pairs will take a heading each and in ICT suite will research their area. Need to make notes to enable them to write a report on their area. By end of Monday's lesson will have two reports and one poster representing each area. Give out prompt sheets to direct their research.

	• By the end of today need to have researched and made notes on area. Decided on newsletter template using Microsoft Publisher, decided on headline and import a picture. On Monday we will review progress, check understanding and write up report. Those doing a poster need to research area, start to consider key points as per sheet so are ready on Monday to design and print poster.
10 mins	Plenary: • Check progress of each area. Share some examples of newsletters on interactive whiteboard. • Summarize progress so far and expectation for Monday.

Vocabulary:

News, issues, country, land use, environmental quality, community, physical features, ordnance survey maps, wind farms, noise pollution, health issues, wind turbine noise, destruction, landscape.

Resources:

- Websites
- Map of area
- Siege campaign leaflet
- Picture of wind farm
- Prompt sheets for less able and independent pairs.

Differentiation:

Six more able children (three Year 5s and three year 6s) will be my focus children. They have already interviewed a teacher who is on the committee against the proposed wind farm. They will also interview a local resident. My expectation of this group is a report with reported speech from both interviews and appropriate quotes representing the local resident's views.

SEN/IEP:

The less able will work in pairs with the teacher's assistant to produce a poster bringing the issue to the attention of children. This group will produce three posters representing the views of three of the concerned parties trying to influence children. The children will have a prompt sheet detailing key areas to consider when designing a poster for children. The class has been paired, using prior knowledge through assessment of ability and personality, to provide appropriate peer support.

The boy who has an IEP for behavioural problems has been paired with a mature, responsible girl, Nicole. They work well together. A positive behaviour management strategy to be employed. Although his IEP states that working on computer is a reward for good behaviour it is expected that ICT will provide its own motivation.

Use of ICT:

The newspaper reports will be written up in Lesson 2 in the ICT suite using Microsoft Publisher.

The less able will produce a poster also in the ICT suite.

It was during the second session that the children produced their final work. Whether they were writing the newsletter or designing a poster, all groups were given a prompt sheet, and examples of these are shown below. After checking that the children had chosen suitable templates, the work was then produced using Microsoft Publisher. The results illustrated that the children were by now well aware of the proposed development and its possible effect on the local environment. This was reinforced during the plenary, in which the children demonstrated that they had understood the arguments for and against the development. Using the interactive whiteboard, each group was represented and their various findings, reports and posters shared with the rest of the class.

Detail	Information	Tick when completed
Title	Is it interesting? Will it entice the reader to read your article? Try to intrigue your reader so that they want to read further.	
Planning	Have you planned it and brainstormed it with your partner? What key information needs to be included? Organize it. Use mind map/spider diagrams.	
Picture	Use a picture which can help to illustrate what you are saying.	
Language	Present tense, general nouns unless reporting an interview. Factual description, technical words and phrases e.g. wind turbine. Formal, impersonal language.	
Audience	Someone who wants to know about the subject. Consider them when writing.	
Writing with a partner	Rehearse, write – one writes, one helps. Reread – does it make sense?	

Figure 1.3 The wind farm newsletter prompt sheet. These were produced by the teacher to prompt the pupils to think about all of the key aspects of the task. It is this attention to detail that ensures a successful lesson.

Figure 1.4 The prompt sheet for the wind farm posters.

Detail	Information	Tick when completed
Colour	Must be bright and eye catching – needs to appeal to children.	
Bold	Easy to read and understand.	
Clear	Think about the font – will it appeal to the children?	
Pictures	Are they the best pictures to help you make your point?	
Appeal to audience	Is it appropriate for the children it is designed for?	
Facts	Are the facts relevant? Will children understand them?	
Appropriate language	Is the language simple but still able to get the view point across? (Use a thesaurus to help.)	

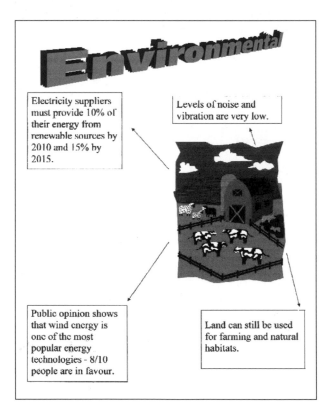

Figure 1.5 A wind farm poster.

COLLINGWOOD ENVIRONMENTAL

Why Wind?

This is an important question which the residents of Southminster are asking at this very moment.

The government has set the Electricity companies a challenging target, they must provide 10% of their energy from renewable sources by 2010. This increases to 15% by 2015.

Targets are necessary because of the urgent need to reduce the greenhouse effect.

Key Facts:

1. Public opinion shows that 8/10 people are in favour of wind energy.
2. Modern Wind turbines produce electricity 70—85% of the time.
3. It is a renewable form of energy.
4. One turbine per year can produce enough electricity to run a computer for 1620 years.

A modern wind turbine is simply an improved model of the original windmill which you often see around our country side.

It produces electricity by working in exactly the opposite way to a fan, instead of using electricity to make wind, the turbines use wind to make electricity.

Building wind farms on land does not prevent the land still being used for farming or by wildlife for their natural habitats. What it does provide is a renewable form of energy helping to supply homes with electricity.

Figure 1.6 A wind farm newsletter.

ARE YOU UP FOR WIND - FARMS

This is a important question that the residensed are asking at this very moment .

8 out of 10 people agree with having wind farms ,and less than 1 out of 10 are against it .A modern wind turbine is simply a improved model of a original wind mill.

Figure 1.7 A wind farm poster

The examples of the planning sheet together with the prompt sheets show just how much care was taken by the teacher to ensure the success of this project. The posters illustrate not only how much the children understood about the importance of developments such as these to local people and their environment, but also confirm that they were able to utilize ICT to support and enhance their work. The pupils were engaged, the more able were stretched and the whole activity was genuinely cross curricular. The less able pupils could also access the learning objectives and were supported by a teaching assistant.

Using an interactive whiteboard

One of the most significant and widespread ICT resources to be developed and introduced into primary schools in the last few years is the interactive whiteboard. As the name suggests, this is a whiteboard that interactively controls and displays content from a host computer via a data projector. Chapter 3 of our previous book, *ICT and Primary Mathematics* devotes an entire chapter to discussing how to use one of these impressive pieces of equipment.

There are three main types of interactive whiteboard on the market, each with increasing amounts of functionality. The most advanced type of board, the Promethean Activboard, operates in three modes. These are:

- *Display* mode, where the board displays the desktop or programs from the host computer, and can be controlled by making inputs using a small pen-like device called a stylus (in a similar way to pointing and clicking with a mouse). This is the simplest form of usage and is probably most useful for demonstrating software to pupils.
- *Annotate over windows* mode, where the Activboard software allows the stylus to write, draw or highlight over the top of the displayed screen content without being able to click on it. This is particularly useful for annotating, perhaps with lines or arrows.
- *Flipchart* mode. This is where the Activboard software displays a series of blank screens, which can then be used in a similar way to a traditional whiteboard. The user can draw lines, shapes or arrows freehand (with lines of different colours and thicknesses), or can write on the board with a function that allows the user's handwriting to be converted into a standard font, which can then be imported into a standard word processing package. Additionally, there is an extensive collection of pre-installed resources and images, which can be drawn by selecting and dragging out to the required size. Called 'Annotations', these resources include angles, arrows, borders, call-outs, scientific, flowchart and logic symbols, as well as maps, shapes and flags. Another useful feature of the flipchart mode is the background and tile options. As the name suggests, this option allows the user to select pre-drawn backgrounds which can then be drawn or written over.

Quite apart from being an excellent tool for the teacher to use to display content and to explain key concepts and ideas, the interactive whiteboard is at its most powerful when being used by the pupils themselves. The latest version of the software that allows the board to be used, Activprimary, has a very child-centric user interface, which is extremely easy and intuitive to use. The authors have seen some outstanding uses of these boards by children, including a group of Foundation Stage pupils using one to read and listen independently to talking story-books, and another group of children sorting out shapes into different groups (depending on their properties) as part of a class lesson on shape and space. In early years classrooms these boards are specially fixed to the wall near the floor to ensure that the children can reach them from the floor.

Paradoxically, in the experience of the authors the interactive whiteboard is least effectively used for discrete ICT lessons! This is because in this capacity it can only be used really in 'point and click' mode – which can be done with a mouse and then projected onto a screen anyway. It is when being used in flipchart mode that it is at its most effective, which largely discounts ICT lessons. However, for subjects such as Art and Design, History, Geography, Music and Modern Foreign Languages, it has the potential to be a revolutionary and invaluable tool. When used in this mode or by the pupils it is an extremely effective use of ICT and as such the teacher needs to consider exactly how it is to be used. If, however, it is used in 'display and explanation mode' by the teacher, it is only a resource, and in the authors' view cannot be considered legitimate use of ICT in supporting a subject.

Clearly, the availability of such a board will have a significant impact upon the planning and the delivery of the lesson. The teacher will need to consider how he or she uses the board, or whether the emphasis should be on letting the children use it.

Summary

The case study detailed above illustrates the importance of careful and detailed planning, but above all, the importance of placing the Foundation Subject first and focusing upon this. It needs to be remembered that ICT is being used in a supporting role rather than as the main focus: the only time that ICT becomes the main focus is when it is taught as a discrete subject. This is not to say that the requirements of the National Curriculum for England cannot be met – the case study above is an excellent example of the 'Communicating and handling information' strand – but it should not be the main focus. When used in this supporting role, ICT can greatly enhance the Foundation Subjects. The following chapters identify in greater detail the opportunities that ICT presents for each of them.

References

DfEE (1999) *National Curriculum, Handbook for Primary Teachers, Key Stages 1 and 2.* DfEE/QCA, London.

DfEE (1998) *High Status, High Standards,* Circular Number 4/98. DfEE, London.

National Advisory Committee on Creative and Cultural Education (1998/9) *All Our Futures: Creativity, Culture, and Education.* DfEE, London.

Williams, J. and Easingwood, N. (2003) *ICT and Primary Science.* RoutledgeFalmer, London.

Useful websites

www.becta.org.uk
British Educational Communications and Technology Agency

www.nc.uk.net
The National Curriculum for England

www.ncaction.org.uk
The National Curriculum in Action

www.qca.org.uk/ages3-14/afl/907.html
The Ten Principles of Assessment, from the Qualifications and Curriculum Authority

www.standards.dfes.gov.uk/primary
The primary strategy website

www.standards.dfes.gov.uk/schemes
The QCA schemes of work website

CD-Roms, programs and useful addresses

The Ask Oscar program can be obtained from Data Harvest Group Ltd, 1 Eden Court, Leighton Buzzard, Bedfordshire, LU7 4FY.

Black Cat Numbers, Words and Pictures 2 is published by Granada Learning Ltd, Granada Television, Quay Street, Manchester, M60 9EA.

The Activboard and Activprimary software are developed by Promethean Limited, Promethean House, Lower Philips Road, Blackburn, Lancashire, BB1 5TH.

2 Design and Technology

Design and technology and the school

Design and Technology is a relatively new subject in the school curriculum. It has evolved from a combination of the old secondary school subjects of woodwork and metalwork with technical drawing. At that time these were not often considered academic subjects and were seldom taught to the academically-inclined pupils. Consequently, they were not given the status which they deserved. Even the first publications of the National Curriculum for England did not include Design and Technology as a separate subject: Technology was one of the sections in the Science document.

This is not surprising. History shows that technology has always been an integral part of the scientific process. Obviously theoretical science is essential: but if it is to progress beyond theory, then the skills and knowledge of technology will be required. In the past, whole civilizations have been built upon the ability to utilize this technology. Ancient China and the Roman Empire are just two examples. On a smaller scale, individual scientists throughout history have turned their hands to technology to help them with their scientific discoveries. For example, both Galileo and Newton built their own telescopes, without which they could never have completed their work.

When the National Curriculum for England was first revised, Technology became a part of the Art syllabus, and it is only relatively recently that, as Design and Technology, it has become a subject in its own right. Obviously this is as it should be, but in primary schools at least there still remains the feeling that it is an art-based subject, despite Art and Design having its own place in the curriculum. This has led in the past to some teachers ignoring many of the essential components of Technology, such as mechanics and electronics, structures and forces, and the basic elements of the science of materials. Making clay models may be Technology, as some technical knowledge is needed to complete them properly: but making simple plasticene models is not, and should be part of the art lesson.

The design process

This describes the stages through which a design project passes from the first ideas to the finished object. It is able to be applied as much to the designing and building of a large aeroplane or ship, as to the smallest and most simple artefact or ornament, and can include the following:

- Needs
- First ideas
- Working drawings
- Chosen idea with plans
- Prototype
- Modifications if necessary
- Marketing if required (including presentation)

We shall say more about the separate stages later in the chapter. For the moment it should be remembered that as with all such examples this is essentially a guide, and should not be interpreted in too rigid a manner, otherwise individual initiative and imagination can be lost.

Design and making

All Technology has to be combined with the Design element of the subject. In the authors' opinion it is better if these two aspects are directly related and not treated as if they were different curriculum subjects. However, this can raise problems if children are first asked to design something that will later be made into a working model. If the designer, in this case a primary school pupil, is going to produce a sketch, working drawing or plan that can then be used to make a working model, he or she must first have some practical technical knowledge of how the model works and how the parts fit together. The authors have often seen drawings produced by children who had been asked to design various vehicles. These should eventually have been used to build working models – but these unfortunately never materialised, as however delightful the drawings, the children had little or no knowledge of the working parts of even a simple toy. They could not, for instance, show how to fit the wheels and axles, or even suggest what materials could be used.

Obviously this example suggests that some previous knowledge is required: but if the 'rule' that design must come before 'making' is rigidly followed, then how is this knowledge to be gained? Perhaps during a Science lesson, or even by leaving the Design part until later, to allow the children to see and handle the different working parts first (for example, they can deconstruct existing models) so that they can explore how they work and fit together. Construction kits can help, and we shall have more to say about these later in the chapter, as well as suggesting further examples that can utilize all the potentialities of Design and making in one continuous process, even for the youngest children.

ICT and design and technology

We have already said that ICT should play an integral part in all subjects; indeed, any area of the curriculum that involves technology can hardly exist without it. Nevertheless, even when so many operations are done by computers, they do not replace the human element. In the adult world of finance, industry or pure science, where the use of the computer is universal, it is nevertheless a human being who operates it. It is a human who feeds it with information, and who decides what it should do with that information. It is even a technician who will mend it when it goes wrong. This is how it should be in the classroom. Even when we use control technology to make a series of machines work at the command of a computer, someone must first feed in the commands and start the process going. It is true that in industry, when ICT has been used on the factory assembly line, it has made many of the 'old' skills redundant. This is something we all need to remember particularly when teaching Design and Technology. However, we should at the same time realise that as those skills were no longer required, new ones for ICT were taking their place. And we also need to remember that as a consequence of this, the data that is entered into a computer and the resultant information is only as good as the human who enters it: GIGO is a popular term amongst the professional ICT community – Garbage In, Garbage Out.

Applying the design process in the primary school

If children are going to do worthwhile topics then the teacher's planning needs to consider several important points:

- Do the children understand that what they design will eventually be made into an actual object? (For the purpose of this chapter we shall take it for granted that this is what the teacher intends, and that the object in question will be a model, perhaps with working parts – or at the very least one that has more than just a decorative use.)
- Do the children have the necessary skills both to design the object, and subsequently construct it?
- Is there a need for the object, or is it just something that they or the teacher have decided upon for other reasons?

'Needs'

It is arguable that some of the best technology arises from a real situation that needs a solution. Supplying a village in Africa with constant access to water, building bridges, roads and dams are obvious examples, although they do all not have to be on such a grand scale. Designing the first wheel was a technological breakthrough, as were perhaps the first knife, fork and spoon or kettle. It is worth remembering at this stage that all these objects, however well and aesthetically designed, should obey scientific and engineering principles. It is no use if the bridge cannot withstand the forces put upon it or a knife cannot cut, however pleasing to the eye it may be. One of the authors has a kettle that, although it has won many design awards, regularly boils over because the spout is in the wrong place. The designer had obviously forgotten the old adage that 'water always finds its own level'.

What part does ICT play in this kind of topic?

To answer this in full it would be appropriate here to describe a topic that one of the authors completed some years ago when he was responsible for a mixed class of top infants (Year 2). It illustrates the complete process, from first designs to completed object (which answered a genuine need at the time). Although we have said that having such a need gives an impetus to a project, we are not suggesting that teachers should manufacture pretend 'needs'. This should not be necessary: for this example will show how a 'need' can arise from other activities within the classroom. It is a simple technological project, but one commensurate with the expertise and experience of the children at that time, and one that illustrates a relatively early use of ICT– in terms of both the development of ICT, and the age of the children.

Box 2.1   Designing and making a 'bird scarer'

As we have said, this project was carried out by a Year 2 class that had little or no previous experience of this kind of work. To enable the children to complete the topic without at this stage having to learn a lot of new technology, a model was needed that although having a practical use, did not have any moving parts. Hence the choice of a bird scarer.

As part of their Science investigations, the children had been planting seeds in containers as well as in the small strip of garden just outside the classroom window. It was felt that it was necessary to protect the growing seeds from birds. It is arguable, of course, that it would be a very brave bird that would go near a class of 30 young children: but any gardener will tell you, particularly in the case of lawn seed, that some protection is often necessary. Certainly the children thought so, and after much discussion they came up with several ideas.

It was at this stage that the computer was first used, albeit by the teacher. Each of the children was given a 'Design Sheet'. For this age it was a simple, computer-designed and produced sheet of A4, which had spaces for their name, and for a short description of the topic. Most importantly it asked the child to write down and sketch their first ideas, and then to pick one of them and explain their choice. Finally, there was a space for a design drawing, or even a rough plan. If a suitable program was available the children could have been given the choice to complete this all on a computer for themselves, not only drawing up the design sheet but also completing it with drawings and plans. Unfortunately, this was not possible at the time, although it has since been done again in this way with older children, using the drawing tools in programs such as Microsoft Word and PowerPoint. Nevertheless, even many of the older children still decided to make the drawings themselves, with pencil or marker pen.

It was decided that their basic design should be a cat's face – for obvious reasons. There is however a valuable teaching point to be made here. We have highlighted the difficulty that children will have if asked to design something without having any previous experience of what they are asked to design, or any knowledge of how it works. But we have yet to meet the child who could not draw a cat's face, however basic the design might be.

Figure 2.1 A cat's face drawn using the drawing tools in Microsoft Word. This was designed using simple shapes and straight lines. It could then be printed and enlarged if necessary!

It is at this stage that the computer was used for the second time, although now by the children themselves. Using the now well known My World program, supplied by Dial Solutions Limited in conjunction with Derbyshire Local Education Authority, they produced a good computer design for their cat, although this could have just as easily been produced with any simple drawing tools (see Figure 2.1). At that time there was only one computer in each classroom and no others in the school, so only two children were able to use it at any one time. This took some organizing but the effort was very worthwhile, not only because of the computer skills that the children acquired, but the motivation it gave them. The organization would be easier today where every school has a bank of several computers in a specialized setting, as well as, we hope, at least two in each classroom. Some of the designs were enlarged to use as 'stick on' templates. Others were kept as ideas for reference.

It can be seen from this case study that even young children benefited from using ICT, albeit at this relatively early stage of its development. It is a simple but complete project incorporating not only ICT but all the stages of the design process. It originated from work that was first carried out as part of the children's Science curriculum, and to some extent involved the children in art and craft work as well as simple drawing. As in much good design and technology, there can be a considerable amount of mathematics. At first this will be mainly simple measurement, but older children might require higher skills such as knowledge of scale, proportion and area.

Finally, in order to understand the prepared design sheets which introduced them to the first concepts of design, the children had to accept new words and phrases, such as, 'designing', 'original', 'plan' and 'working drawing'. Incidentally, the authors have found that children enjoy using design sheets for all such projects. The children seem to attach great importance to them, which provides motivation and interest, particularly if they design the sheets themselves. They feel more involved – or perhaps it is that they consider that they are doing 'grown up' work.

Summary of this project

Discussion

Need to protect seeds from birds.

First ideas – first use of ICT

- Arising from the initial discussion these were either sketched on design sheets or produced on computer.
- Accepted idea (cat's face) drawn on card or larger template stuck on card and both cut out.
- Further design work on the cat's face complete with normal feline features as well as additions to make the face an effective bird scarer (such as the addition of strips of silver foil). This entailed more work on the computer using My World although there are now several suitable art based programs available such as 2Simple's Draw or Black Cat's Fresco.
- Completed faces fixed in place hanging from canes amongst the seeds and seedlings.
- Observation – no birds therefore seeds safe!

Design and the use of ICT

We have described a design project carried out several years ago, when ICT was in its infancy. With the hardware and software now available to schools, there can be no reason why most design work of whatever topic can not be carried out on the computer, with the important proviso that children still need to acquire the basic skills of drawing. These may be learned in their Art lessons, but drawing should also at least be a part of the children's first design ideas.

As we have suggested, at its best technology in the primary school should be of a 'hands on' practical kind: therefore, during the actual making of the model the computer may not always have much of an input. However, this is more than made up for in the design stage. In our two books (*ICT and Primary Science* and *ICT and Primary Mathematics*), we have tried to show how ICT is invaluable in the teaching of those subjects, but have nevertheless stressed the essential practical work on which much of the computer work is based. This is also the case with Design and Technology, but with one major difference. In Science much of the ICT involves listing and recording work already carried out in the field or classroom, albeit followed by the very important analysis of this information. Similar recording of data can be a part of Mathematics, although the computer is often used to help with or indeed carry out various calculations. This work often involves database and particularly spreadsheet type programs. For control technology, computers will be programmed to make the completed technology work. However, it is at the design stage, before children actually start to make the model or artefact, that the computer can first be used, even when the model is not part of a control technology project.

Design skills

Children should be encouraged to complete as much of their design work using a computer as current software allows. Although we have previously suggested that the first ideas, rough sketches, and even good detailed presentational drawings can be done by hand, ideally a combination of ICT together with their own art work is often more appropriate. The authors have been pleasantly surprised to find that many designers still incorporate hand-drawn sketches and layouts in their work, even when they have invested large sums of money in modern hard and software. It seems that they often need to sketch out by hand their original ideas, as well as to see just how these ideas look on a completed page. It seems that even designers of computer web pages often need to do this, and so they lay much emphasis on the importance of learning 'hands-on' drawing and colouring skills at an early age. The presentational drawing, which comes at the end of the whole process, is of particular importance if the children are doing a marketing project.

Marketing projects

These projects, while involving all aspects of Design and Technology, also include the additional requirements for marketing the product, such as costing, pricing, presentation and perhaps even advertising. These may be simple topics which involve making small artefacts to be sold for school funds at the summer or Christmas sale, or they can be more ambitious projects, which involve making toys, simple musical instruments or stuffed animals, again to be sold at the appropriate time. It can also include making cakes, biscuits, sandwiches and other similar foods. In one school we know of it involved the class in preparing and presenting a complete three-course meal.

Whatever the chosen product, the children should be involved from the very beginning. The need for the product is obvious, designs and recipes have to be prepared, models and foods have to be made, and all with the intention that they will be sold to parents and visitors. Health and safety issues need to be taken into account, as does the marketing aspect. This will require suitable presentation (where the children's drawing and artistic skills will be paramount), as well as the all-important costing of the product. This latter will involve some cross-curricular mathematical skills, and can also include some other aspects of good ICT, such as the use of spreadsheets.

Using spreadsheets and databases: cross-curricular activities

While it is unlikely that database programs will be needed in Design and Technology, spreadsheets are invaluable where any costing process is required, such as in the marketing projects described above. For example, using a four column spreadsheet, the names of the items can be listed in the first column, with their individual costs in the second, and the quantity of each item in the third column. The spreadsheet can be configured to multiply the costs in columns two and three to display the answer in the fourth. It can then add all the item costs of column four to give a total cost in the cell at the bottom right corner. In this way children can apply their numeracy skills to practical problems. Costs of individual ingredients for baking cakes or biscuits, as against their total cost, together with prices and profit margins can all be calculated in this way.

Drawing plans

Whether it is for a simple 'one-off' artefact, a controlled model, or one of the many objects for a marketing project, a good computer program is ideal for the actual scale plan or working drawing. This will not only allow the children to make clear and accurate diagrams, it will take into account scale, size, and even area. It will also enable them to make changes to their drawings as they progress, and correct any mistakes they might make. Programs like Black Cat's Designer or a computer's own design program such as Microsoft Draw enable children to benefit from all that the computer has to offer, in a similar way that a database program will produce the graphs, pie charts and scattergrams that result from the children's previous investigations in other subjects.

Using appropriate design programs children can produce clear and accurate working drawings or plans (Figure 2.2). To test just how good they are, the designs should be able to be used by somebody other than the pupil who drew them. Producing plans, instructions, or even recipes that others can follow is not easy, but it is a necessary skill (and one that some in commerce and industry have yet to acquire). An interesting example of how difficult this can be, and one moreover that uses construction kits to good advantage, is to ask a pupil to construct a simple model, such as a car or aeroplane. These can be very basic models, but the pupil should then be asked to write a list of instructions to explain how this model is made. There is no reason why this should not be done by computer. These instructions are then given to another pupil who is asked to use them to rebuild the model – not an easy task!

Three interactive CD-Roms suitable for Key Stage Two – Design and Technology

- Mechanical Toys (2003)
- Fairground Rides (2004)
- Design and Create (2005)

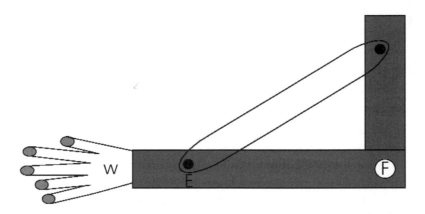

Figure 2.2 Arm made of card with elastic-band 'muscle' produced using the drawing tools of Microsoft Word. The arm is a third type lever: W=Weight, E= Effort, F=Fulcrum. This is an inefficient lever: would it be possible to have an arm designed as a more efficient first or second type lever?

These three programs are published by Focus Educational Software Ltd., and can be obtained either directly from them or from Technology Teaching Systems (see page 65). The first, Mechanical Toys, is specifically designed as a teaching aid research program to enable students to understand simple mechanics through reference to a range of simple mechanical toys. There are 21 examples of various automata that show, among other things, different types of motion, cams, levers, pulley and gear systems. The program also includes an on-screen test facility, a module which analyses the motion of cams, and most important, a 2D drawing program that allows students to design their own models.

The second program, Fairground Rides, is designed to complement the QCA Unit 6C – 'Fairground'. There are 18 different 'rides', which are described using 3D animations, photographs, videos and text. There are sections that explain many of the mechanisms described above, but also include electrical circuits and switching. This is an interactive program which allows the student to assemble and test various circuits and switches on screen. This CD-Rom also includes a 2D design program.

For the primary school, Design and Create is probably the program most suited to whole class project work, as it enables pupils to experience the complete process of designing and making. This CD-Rom covers seven QCA schemes of work. It is fully animated, with three distinct modes that combine some material shown in the previous two CD-Roms: but in addition it contains much of what the experienced teacher will recognize as 'traditional' primary construction work.

Pupils can begin with the teaching mode, where they can choose any of seven topics such as 'Moving Pictures', 'Playgrounds', 'Vehicles', or 'Photo frames' and 'Homes'. With the exception of the last two examples, all the models are chosen to show the various mechanisms that form the basis of much technology. For example, 'Moving Pictures' illustrates sliding mechanisms, 'Playgrounds' shows rotary mechanisms such as round-abouts, and 'Vehicles' explains wheel bearings and lever mechanisms. Others, such as 'Winding Up', give examples of water wells and windmills, while 'Moving Monsters' illustrates a dragon's head with moving parts.

For this teaching mode all the models shown are made from construction kits. The models can be made to move, and by using the various icons the pupil will see how the models are assembled. For the construction mode the models are also based on construction kits, but it also contains several other alternative programs. For example, by clicking on the 'Photo' icon followed by 'Project Library', the pupil can be shown a series of models for each topic, any of which can be made in the primary classroom.

These models are constructed from either standard construction materials such as card wheels, dowels, cotton reels and jig-made dowel and card cogs, or so called 'found' materials, such as plastic bottles and cardboard boxes. These are the 'traditional' primary models mentioned earlier, and the authors are delighted to see that they still form the basis of so much good primary Design and Technology. Indeed, some of the models (such as the monster with a mouth that will open when a balloon is inflated), together with some of the vehicles, winding mechanisms and houses, remind them of models illustrated in books written by one of the authors several years ago. (Williams, 1991 and 1997.)

The 'Design and Create' CD-Rom also contains two programs that allow for design work. Within the construction mode, the 'Photos' option not only includes the project library described above, but also contains an introduction, which gives detailed step-by-step illustrated instructions on how to draw a variety of objects and animals – we particularly like the cat. However, the third and final mode consists of an entire design program that offers a wide choice of 'ready made' drawings on which to base working models, and more importantly it allows the pupil to produce their own designs. For these the pupil can use a complete range of lines, colours, shadings and shapes, and a variety of drawing tools.

Throughout this book the authors have suggested a variety of programs suitable for many subjects. Some, like PowerPoint, are an obvious choice to illustrate various projects, often from their very beginnings. Others, such as a database or spreadsheet program, should form an integral part of many scientific, geographical or even mathematical investigations. Programs like the three described above are an essential part of the processes of Design and Technology. They enable pupils to investigate how the mechanisms and structures of technology work, and then help them to design a working model. Finally, and perhaps most importantly, the programs enable the pupils to build their chosen model, often incorporating moving parts or even an electrical circuit, while at the same time enhancing their ICT skills by the actual use of the program itself.

Box 2.2 Designing nets

One of the most basic yet essential design and make activities (DMA) for primary age children is the construction of three-dimensional boxes from two dimensional shapes, or nets. This is a key skill which in turn can be scaled up and transferred to a wide range of mathematical and Design and Technology contexts, and create some interesting science investigations, such as the very important ratio between an organism's volume and its surface area (Lambert and Williams ,1987). It is an example of a cross-curricular project that involves learning necessary computer skills to produce three dimensional shapes to be used for work in other subjects, but that still requires simple making skills such as cutting, and perhaps some further art work.

Designing nets lends itself ideally to being completed on a computer and provides a simple yet dynamic example of how ICT can be employed to support various areas of the curriculum using everyday software. The use of the drawing tool functions of Microsoft Word or PowerPoint captures the interactivity, speed and automatic function and provisionality that the computer offers without the need to invest in expensive and occasionally used specialist CAD/CAM software. Once the children have constructed the net on the screen they can then model different shapes and alter the position of the tabs through the use of the cut/copy and paste functions. This can also be demonstrated by the children or the teacher dragging the net's component shapes around the screen using an interactive whiteboard, to provide group or whole class interactive demonstrations.

Producing a net for a cube

The net is produced by drawing one square using the drawing tools, which are located on the drawing toolbar in Microsoft Word and PowerPoint. When dragging the square out, the shift key should be held as this will ensure that the shape remains square throughout sizing. Once the desired size has been reached, the square is then highlighted and copied once, and is then pasted five times. It is important to ensure that the square is not too small for the children to cut out, but also it should not be too large, as four squares' length plus tabs will need to fit onto an A4 page for printing. The squares are then dragged and dropped into the required position. The 'Snap to grid' option needs to be turned on to ensure that each square fits exactly against the next one. This is found in 'Grids and Guides' under the 'View' menu.

The tabs are then added (Figure 2.3). Again, this is done by drawing and filling one tab using the drawing tools, then copying and pasting the required number of times. The tabs will also need to be rotated into the correct plane. This is done by highlighting and rotating using the circular green 'handle'. The real challenge for the children here is to get them to try to work out where a tab needs to go in order for the box to be successfully glued together. The teacher can ask interactive yet focused questions such as, "Are all of the tabs in the correct place? If not, where should they be?" The children can also model different designs of nets by experimenting with the squares in different positions, or even changing some of the squares to produce a range of shapes. An additional challenge could be provided by adding images to the sides of the finished box – which would mean calculating which orientation the image would need to be in on the net. Again, images are rotated by highlighting and dragging with the handle.

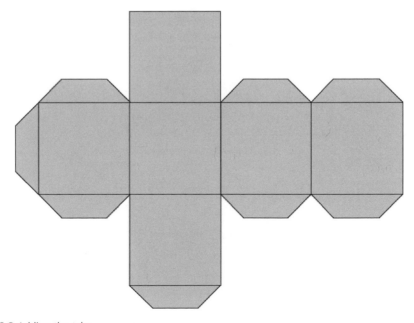

Figure 2.3 Adding the tabs

Producing a net for a square-based box

The square can remain the same size, but rectangles can now be used to form a square-based box. If a lid were to be added, where would it be positioned? What shape and size would it need to be? How could it be produced quickly and accurately? And again, are all of the tabs necessary?

Producing a net for a pyramid

The rectangular sides can then be replaced with isosceles triangles to produce a net for a pyramid (Figure 2.4). This is produced from the original net by deleting all of the squares apart from one, and drawing and filling one triangle. One tab is extended and rotated and fixed to the side of the triangle. By holding down the shift key, both the triangle and the tab can be highlighted simultaneously and be grouped using the 'Group' option in the 'Draw' menu to create one object. This was then copied and pasted a further three times, before being dragged and dropped into the correct position. It was of course necessary to rotate each object before positioning, and the 'Snap to grid' option should be turned off. Use of the 'Nudge' tool ensures a perfect join.

Producing a net for a triangular prism

This is a little more complicated, as the triangle sides needs to be the same length as the rectangle ends in order for it to fit together properly. This is designed by producing a rectangle, copying it and pasting it twice before dragging and dropping into the correct position. Two equilateral triangles need to be drawn, tabs added and located as appropriate. But the tabs can be positioned in several different ways. Can you suggest any variations?

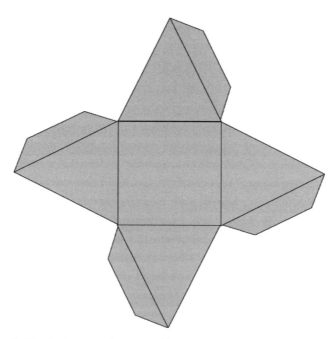

Figure 2.4 Producing a net for a pyramid

Control technology

We devoted a chapter to this topic in our book, *ICT and Primary Science*. As we stated in the introduction to this chapter, there are many direct links between Technology and Science, and we therefore felt that it had a place in that book. However, as control technology is part of the Design and Technology curriculum in most schools (and indeed the National Curriculum for England), it would be wrong not to include it here, and particularly as it is the one area that Ofsted feels has been overlooked in primary schools. This can hardly be because of a lack of resources, although it may be that some teachers lack the knowledge and therefore confidence to teach it. It may also be that, because it is a time-consuming activity, teachers do not feel that they have enough space in a crowded timetable. We hope that we can show not only how important and relevant control technology is in today's classroom, but how the time spent teaching it can be utilized to include all aspects of Design and Technology, as well as ICT and many other subjects. Control technology not only involves a computer as the controlling element, but also ICT as part of the whole process in the designing and making of the model to be controlled. At its best, this model could include levers, pulleys, gearing and sliding mechanisms, and of course a variety of electrical circuits.

The first stages in control

When making models, particularly those including electrical circuits, it will in most cases be the children themselves who set them working. Even when an outside agent is responsible for starting their models, this is likely to be a natural element such as wind or water. However, there are many examples outside the classroom of machines that are not directly controlled by hand. Children may make lighthouses complete with bulbs and batteries and a switch, which they will operate. They may make level-crossing barriers or simple water-raising devices that both work in a similar way, based on the principle of the first-type lever. However, in life how many of these machines are now worked by hand? The water-raising device perhaps, as these are more often found in remote villages of Africa and India: but the others very seldom indeed. Most are remote-controlled and are triggered by other means. These could be a timed switch or a light sensitive cell or perhaps a pressure pad. Most children will have stood before the sliding doors of a supermarket waiting for them to open, with probably a good idea of how they work. All the more reason why they should be given the chance to learn more about it in the classroom.

We have already mentioned the automated assembly line as being an example of control technology in industry, while sliding doors and to some extent the automatic level crossings are ones that children will have experienced themselves. One of the authors came across an interesting domestic use of control technology while he was on holiday. The house in which he and his wife were staying was equipped with an automatic sprinkler system. At a given time the sprinklers would rise up from grass level and for a half hour or so water the garden, moving from side to side as they did so. There were three sets of sprinklers each working in turn, one after the other. There was a bank of computers in the garage to work these, as well as the automatic garage doors. There must have been a complex set of instructions for these computers, for they would need a command to switch the sprinklers on, with perhaps an automatic mechanism to raise and lower them incorporated within this. They would also have needed a command to turn the water on and off, and probably repeat commands for each of the three sets.

We have described this in some detail because it is a model for the kind of control technology that children can do. It is not our intention to duplicate the control technology chapter of our previous book: however, it is necessary to describe how children can make use of their designing and making skills for control technology.

Box 2.3 Making and controlling a simple level crossing barrier

We have already said something about designing, so for this example we can take it that the children will have already completed this stage. They will make the barrier (Figure 2.5) from a length of 1cm square section wood (we know that centimetres are not S.I. units, but they are a too convenient measurement for us to ignore). A hole is drilled about two centimetres from one end, through which a short length of dowel is passed. Each end of the dowel is put into holes drilled into two other short lengths of square section wood, which act as upright supports glued to a piece of card. The other end of the long square section wood rests on a single upright also stuck to card. If drilling holes in this wood proves to be too difficult then soft balsa wood of a similar size can be used with a thick mapping pin replacing the dowel rod. If the children are used to making these models they will not only recognise this as a first type lever with a fulcrum or balancing point between the load and the effort, but might even have already made something similar. Perhaps one of the water raising devices that we have described and are still in use in many parts of the world.

Figure 2.5 A simple diagram of the barrier, drawn using the drawing tools of Microsoft Word. Children can insert measurements and labels, and they can also change the colours either of the actual drawing or of the background.

As with all these kinds of models, at this stage it can be worked by hand. However, to make it into an example of control technology, it will need to be fitted with an electrical circuit so that it can be opened and closed automatically. A small electro-magnet should be fitted just below the short end of the barrier and a drawing pin fixed to that end of the barrier itself. When the electricity is switched on the electro-magnet is activated, thus attracting the drawing pin, and so the barrier is raised. When the magnet is switched off the barrier is closed as it will fall back under its own weight.

Using the control box

Control technology of this kind requires a control box connected to the computer equipped with the necessary software. On one side of the control box is a set of 'input' terminals, which carry the commands from the computer program, while opposite these are an equal number of 'output' terminals. The 'outputs' can be such things as bulbs, buzzers, or switches of various kinds, and form part of the model.

The children will need to decide what they want their model to do. In the case of the level crossing they might decide to have as many as four 'outputs'. The electromagnetic switch will be one but they can also incorporate two bulbs – one green and one red – as well as a warning buzzer. It will now be necessary for the children to work out the correct sequence in which these 'outputs' work. It might look something like this –

- *Buzzer sounds* (to warn pedestrians)
- *Red light on* (this is to stop traffic going on the level crossing before the barrier comes down)
- *Green light on* (This is for the train)
- *Switch off the electromagnetic switch so barrier comes down*
- *Train passes* (This can be simulated or have a real model train)
- *Green light off*
- *Switch on electromagnetic switch so barrier is raised*
- *Red light off*

In order to turn this into a language that the computer will understand, it will be necessary to know the correct 'command' words. These can vary with different programs, but once you have the appropriate program box on the screen you can then enter the commands in the correct sequence. We use here an example that has been available to schools for several years and can be used with almost all computers found in primary schools. Using the correct commands the program will now look like this:

```
SWITCH ON 1        (the buzzer)
WAIT 5
SWITCH OFF 1
SWITCH ON 2        (the red light)
WAIT 5             (time for foot passengers to cross)
SWITCH ON 3        (the green light)
SWITCH OFF 4       (the electromagnetic switch)
WAIT 20            (or however long it takes for the train to pass)
SWITCH OFF 3
SWITCH ON 4
SWITCH OFF 2
```

Despite appearances, this is a relatively simple set of commands. It does not include a 'REPEAT' command as this is not a continuous procedure, as it would be for example for a lighthouse, which in reality would need to last at least a complete night. There is no 'WAIT UNTIL INPUT IS OFF' type command. This would be used to trigger the sequence when for instance the train passed a light sensor (which would be on) before it reached the level crossing. In this case the appropriate command would go at the very beginning of the sequence. It would be an interesting teaching point for the children to consider if they could in some way make use of the 'on' electro-magnetic switch for this, even if it meant changing the sequence. Finally, we have not incorporated an 'END PROCEDURE' command, which might or might not be required.

We have mentioned construction kits early in the chapter, and if it is not possible to make the level crossing described above with an electromagnetic switch, then children could make one from such a kit using a gearing mechanism. They would still require a high level of skill, for they would need to understand how gears work – particularly worm gears, as these are often an integral part of the construction kit mechanism. They could use their own set of gears made from cotton reels, dowel and rubber bands set within a wooden frame. If they can make these they would certainly understand the principles of gearing. The gears would be worked in conjunction with an electric motor, and therefore the children would also need to have experienced these so that they could enter the correct commands (as the program would be very different from the previous example). Comparing different programs, which complete a similar process but use different mechanisms, is itself a valuable learning experience.

This second command program would look like this –

```
SWITCH ON 1        (buzzer)
WAIT 5
SWITCH OFF 1
SWITCH ON 2        (red light)
WAIT 5
SWITCH ON 3        (green light)
MOTOR ON           (the motor is connected to two outputs to allow the polarity to
                   be reversed – forwards and backwards. The children will need
                   to have found out previously, by trial and error, just how long it
                   needs to run to raise and lower the barrier, and what power the
                   motor needs – this can be fed into the program)
WAIT 5             (the possible time taken to lower the barrier)
MOTOR OFF
WAIT 20
SWITCH OFF 3
MOTOR ON           (it will need to be reversed as the barrier is now being raised –
                   there is a command for this)
SWITCH OFF 2
END PROCEDURE
```

This approach to control technology involves all the processes involved in Design and Technology. There would have been a need for the level crossing in the first place, and this would have been followed by discussion, questioning, ideas, rough sketches, detailed plans, making the model (and the same procedures would have been followed even with the construction kit model), testing by hand or with a simple dry battery, and finally its installation and programming.

Obviously this is a time-consuming process, but surely the children would at least have had experience of design as well as the construction of models from their first years of schooling? A project like this would make a complete and thorough topic for the end of Year 6. However, if this approach is not possible, perhaps because of time or the available resources, teachers have other options, which will also allow the children to learn about control technology with a computer.

Using ready-made models

One such approach is to use a ready-made model – traffic lights, for example – with the control box described above; or a construction kit can be used, complete with its own program and control box. Nowadays these programs usually employ a graphical user interface (GUI), rather than the LOGO-style series of typed command lines, thus providing a range of easily understood icons, and all that the children need do is to click on them to make the model work. While the computer can be used simply as an on/off switch, it is better if the icons are used to program the model to work to a set of commands. These ready-made models can be purchased separately, or can be an addition to the box itself.

Using an on-screen mimic

Although it is clearly desirable for pupils to use 'real' models when creating control sequences, this is not always possible, due to time constraints or limited resources. Even if the pupils make their own models, there will still be a time and cost factor involved. The latest version of the Commotion software, CoCo2, provides the user with an on-screen mimic, which simulates a real situation. This is structured in five stages, with the first stage being suitable for Key Stage 1 children and the later stages being suited to the top end of Key Stage 2. This is illustrated below.

Box 2.4   The car park barrier mimic

The following procedure or program is entered:

```
Begin <entry>
   Repeat forever
     Wait until Input 1 is on
     Turn Motor A on
     Wait for 1 second
     Turn Motor A off
     Wait until Input 4 is on
     Turn Motor A backwards
     Wait for 1 second
     Turn Motor A off
   End Repeat
End <entry>
```

When the procedure is run, the car approaches the barrier, while another car also approaches the barrier to leave. As the first car leaves, it breaks a beam, which allows the second car to enter the car park.

This can also be written as a flow diagram, using standard information system symbols. Children can draw their own flow charts to illustrate virtually any activity, from mixing paints to make a specific colour to describing a journey where more than one kind of transport is used. They need to remember that certain shapes in the chart represent specific commands. The very important diamond-shaped decision box, for example, is used when there is a choice to make between two distinct alternatives. For a flow chart there can be no open-ended questions.

Alternative examples of control technology

Another example of control software is the Robolab package (as described in detail elsewhere). It is often installed in primary school computers and can be used with the Lego Mindstorms equipment. This has a separate Lego brick that contains the control box. It is an entirely separate unit with its own inputs and outputs, and is equipped with wheels so it can be used as a self-contained robot vehicle. Unlike a static control box it is not wired to the computer, but is worked by infra-red signals.

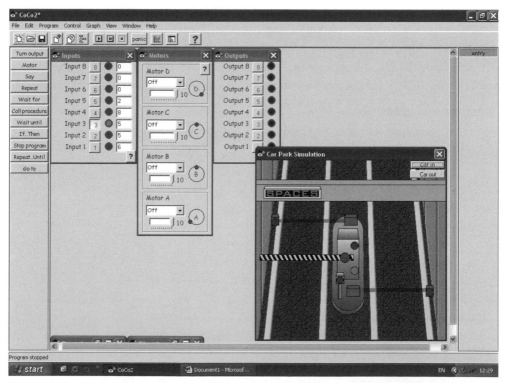

Figure 2.6:The Car Park Barrier mimic in CoCo2. The inputs and outputs are clearly shown on the screen, with the mimic on the right hand side.

The programs are organized in easy stages. Pilot One introduces the children to the icons that work the motors and give simple directional commands, while Pilot Two allows for a change in motor speed and further commands for timing as well as direction. By the time children use Pilot Three, they are able to use a sequence of commands together with other icons so that they can make their robot vehicle follow a carefully planned pathway. It is important that the children understand what the icons mean, so that when they are planning a program they understand what it is they are asking the computer to do. This will not only help them understand the general concept of computer control, but will enable them to build up a useful program with the correct sequence of icons.

Another method by which children can learn about control technology is by using a computer interface such as Flowgo. This kind of interface box allows children to control models using the appropriate software via a computer, or the box can itself act as the controller. The program can be downloaded to the box, which has its own built-in memory. Children can even learn about control technology without ever controlling an actual model: software such as Flowol shows simulated examples (such as crossing lights). It then enables children to build a control program using its own set of commands. These are listed on the screen in a flow chart, which is in itself a very valuable teaching exercise, for it brings a mathematical element into the process. Children should be encouraged to design flow charts as part of their Mathematics lessons. Any operation can be displayed as a flow chart (and we have given some examples in our book *ICT and Primary Mathematics*). They are particularly appropriate for designing command programs, and this software shows clearly why there are differently shaped command boxes, and what kind of command each shape represents.

Teachers need to decide at what level the technology should be. Like all subjects this will depend on the previous experience of the children – and indeed of the teachers. Obviously, controlling models that are first made by the children themselves is often more appropriate for the older children – but the younger ones should also be given the opportunity to construct models, albeit simpler and not intended for control. For while we realize that control simulation programs may well be necessary in today's crowded curriculum, at some period during their time at primary school children must be given the opportunity to design and make actual working models, even if they are not to be used for control technology. However, we envisage the possibility that as the younger children design and make their models they also from time to time visit the computer to learn about control by using either the kit version or the simulated exercise (both described above). In this way, as they mature the children will be able to combine the two skills of construction and computer control.

There must be a natural progression of learning in all subjects, and this progression is perhaps at its most obvious when technical skills are considered. Control technology has a very structured hierarchy all its own (Philip Stephenson, 1997), and in his summary of this progression he lists the processes in relation to commands given to a model robot.

Control technology for younger children

To conclude this section on control we would suggest that model robots should be used to introduce the very youngest children to the process of control technology. A self-contained robot such as a 'Roamer' should be familiar to all primary school teachers: it can be used to enhance Mathematics teaching, often in conjunction with computer screen 'turtles', as well as acting as a precursor to control. For even younger children, there are various simple floor robots available, such as the TTS Bee-Bot. This is illustrated by Figure 2.7 below.

These robots rely on a series of basic commands such as FORWARD, BACK, RIGHT or LEFT (to turn them in those directions). There are often no measurements involved, but only arbitrary numbers, so at the start the children will not know how far the robot will travel with a command such as FORWARD 5. This does not matter: they will find out by trial and error, and can even make lists of distances travelled with certain unit commands such as FORWARD 5 or FORWARD 10. Even more interesting is the command to turn. RIGHT 1 is a natural command to make, but in practice is hardly noticeable. Once they realize that RIGHT 90 represents a quarter turn, then they are on their way to understanding some quite advanced concepts. It is in this way that children begin with simple isolated commands, but soon progress to repeat commands, musical sounds and flashing lights, and therefore eventually to the quite complex systems that we have described.

Data-logging

Although this is not strictly control technology, and will be discussed in much greater depth in the Geography chapter, it needs to be mentioned here as it involves computers with control boxes and a set of sensors that resemble the inputs and outputs of control

technology. Indeed, sensors can be directly linked to control technology, for as inputs they can sense changes in the environment that are recognized by the computer, which is itself programmed to create a linked and corresponding response from the outputs of a control interface box. These could be to close a window or switch on the central heating when the temperature drops below a certain level. There are a variety of these sensors, but the ones most often used in primary schools are those that log temperature, light and sound. These need not be immediately connected to the computer, but can connect to a simple independent piece of equipment, which collects electronically all the data from the sensors. Once this has been done, it can be linked to the computer, which downloads and displays the collected information.

Figure 2.7 The Bee-Bot from TTS. This is a programmable toy, which is moved by entering commands via the buttons on the top. A floor mat can also be purchased to drive the Bee-Bot along! (*Picture courtesy of TTS*)

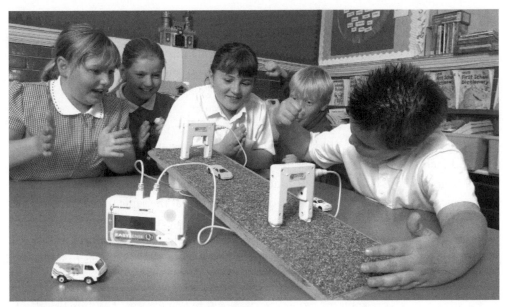

Figure 2.8 Children using the EasySense Data logger from Data Harvest. Here toy cars are timed running down a ramp. As the car passes through the top gate, the logging begins, and ends as it passes through the lower gate. The data can then be downloaded to a computer and the results can be displayed as a graph. (*Picture courtesy of Data Harvest Limited*)

One such piece of equipment is the EcoLog system produced by Data Harvest, consisting of a small interface box, leads, and a set of curriculum notes, together with its software Sensing Science. There are three analogue sensors for measuring the air temperature, light, and sound levels. Once programmed these sensors continually collect the information to be analysed, collated and displayed. In this way a continuous record is kept of any required set of conditions, such as those of an animal habitat or a simple insulation experiment. There is no need for children to take independent occasional records 'by hand', for they can visit the computer at any time for the latest data available. They can collect this information as a graph, which shows all the information in a variety of forms.

While data-logging should be an important technology for many Science projects, other subjects can also benefit from its use. As we will describe later, it can even be used in History (albeit in a rather specialized way). Although it is undoubtedly a very valuable tool in many Science projects, one subject that can most benefit from data-logging with the computer is Geography, as we will hope to show in that chapter.

Food technology

This may not always be a subject on a school's timetable, although in England it is in the National Curriculum as part of Design and Technology. If the school has the choice it might consider it a valuable option when any form of cooking is in progress, or as part of the marketing projects described earlier.

It is an interesting fact that at the time of writing there is much speculation about the nation's diet in general, and school food in particular. Obesity is now considered almost a form of illness, and there is much evidence that this is the result of so called 'junk food'. Ironically, most of this kind of food is the result of highly technological processes. It could be labelled as 'design food', in that the ingredients are very carefully monitored to produce mechanically the most cost-effective product. Conversely, there are other more healthy foods which can owe just as much to technology but pay more attention to what the body really needs, to say nothing of what our tastebuds require.

Food technology is not cooking. It might be a small part of it, although we doubt that any good cook, interested in producing imaginative, fine-tasting meals, would like to be called a food technologist. It is no coincidence that at the same time as the nation's diet is under review, so is the possibility of reintroducing cooking as an essential part of the school curriculum.

While we would welcome its return, it is doubtful if ICT would need to be part of teaching cooking, except perhaps to produce colourful menus and recipes. These could be produced in Microsoft Word or Publisher, and recipes could be displayed as a step-by-step storyboard, as well as in the more traditional manner. Younger children could use 2Publish, part of the excellent Infant Video Toolbox from 2Simple Software, which enables children to draw each stage of the making process and write a sentence underneath each picture. The children could even video themselves making food and then edit it afterwards, complete with voiceovers and music – perhaps in the style of *Ready Steady Cook!* Modern ICT allows children of all ages to record and subsequently edit their work in this way.

However, as opposed to cooking in food technology, there is plenty of scope for the use and development of ICT. Databases can be used to list and identify pupils' most and least favourite foods. PowerPoint presentations can show how food is prepared and displayed, and spreadsheets used to list and calculate the cost of ingredients. For instance, in a long-term marketing project, in which pupils make a study of suitable ingredients for a simple food product, such as a sandwich, and calculate its cost, including packaging, within a given sum of money, all the above uses of ICT are relevant. In such a topic there are obvious links with other subjects.

Cross-curricular links

The part that Design and Technology plays in other subjects, and the opportunity for the teacher to establish imaginative links with these subjects, is surely self-evident. Even before any technology as such is attempted, the design stage must require skills that are often developed in Art, be they simple drawing skills, or more advanced work on shade and light and perspective. A considerable amount of Mathematics is required for measurement, for drawing, recognizing and interpreting graphs and flow charts, and even sometimes for proportion and scale. Much Science needs to be understood when designing and later making working models, and finally, as we have indicated, there are interesting connections with History and Geography. Even food technology has its links with other subjects, such as mathematics and science, for how else can you weigh out ingredients and know what they contain? Likewise, Geography will be needed to identify where various products originate, and the History of nutrition has its place. If the pupils are finding out just what healthy eating means, then even PE may need to be considered. All these give ample opportunities for the relevant and imaginative use of ICT.

References

DfES/QCA (1999) *The National Curriculum for England*, HMSO, London.

Stephenson, P. (1997) *Information Technology and Authentic Learning* (chapter 5), ed. A. MacFarlane. Routledge, London.

Ofsted, *ICT in Schools, A Progress Report* (HMI 4, 23). Ofsted, London.

Williams, J . (1991) *Starting Technology – Machines*. Wayland, Hove.

Williams, J. (1997) *Design and Make – Water Projects*. Wayland, Hove.

Williams, J. and Easingwood, N. (2003) *ICT and Primary Science*, RoutledgeFalmer, London.

Williams, J. and Easingwood, N. (2004) *ICT and Primary Mathematics – A Teacher's Guide*. RoutledgeFalmer, London.

CD-Roms, programs and useful addresses

The Black Cat graphics and art program Fresco is published by Granada Learning Ltd. Granada Television, Quay Street, Manchester, M60 9EA.

The 2Simple software mentioned in the text is published by 2Simple, Enterprise House, 2 The Crest, Hendon, London, NW4 2HN.

Other software as well as a range of materials for design and technology can be obtained from various suppliers such as Technology Teaching Systems, Nunn Brook Road, Huthwaite, Sutton-in-Ashfield, Nottinghamshire, NG17 2HU.

The Mechanical Toys, Fairgrounds, and Design and Create CD-Roms can be obtained either from Technology Teaching Systems, or from Focus Educational Software Ltd (www.focuseducational.com).

Art and Design

Art or design?

On the face of it, Art and Design seem to be two very different subjects, and one also wonders how the 'design' element in this differs from that in Design and Technology. The answer surely is that the techniques of design do not differ. However, in 'Art and Design' it is perhaps *what* we are designing which is different, rather than *how*, particularly when we include craft as part of it. For this reason in this chapter we will treat Art and Design separately, for although obviously there are occasions when they can and do overlap, we would argue that they nevertheless originate from very different points of view. We have no wish to become bogged down with unnecessary subject definitions. It seems that these are only required when devising a written curriculum: therefore to do so here would seem truly pedantic.

Art

It would surely be foolish in the extreme to try to define what is, or what is not art. It is certainly easier to decide what art you like: but it is very dangerous (in the light of history) to deny even the extremes of contemporary art. It is much better to keep an open mind and remember that Constable, a painter who many people consider to be very conventional, was castigated for painting falling drops of water. How could he, it was asked, paint something so momentary? He was of course 'catching the fleeting moment', something that would be taken for granted nowadays. Indeed, the history of art is full of examples that show that almost any new style of painting or sculpture causes problems for the artists concerned. At the very least they have faced ridicule: at worst imprisonment or actual bodily harm! John Sell Cotman of the Norwich School died in obscurity, although his paintings are highly regarded now. Van Gogh during his lifetime only sold one painting – and that to his brother! The impressionists suffered at least verbal abuse, and even today many people are not at all 'sure' about artists like Picasso.

Children and art

At least children need not suffer these problems. We should be happy to allow them to use their unrestricted imaginations, and to experiment both with what they paint or sculpt, and with what materials they use. Obviously in the primary school their choice of materials may be more limited, but they can still learn many of the techniques used by artists, and experiment with these to produce some very sophisticated artwork. By this, we do not mean that children's ideas of art should be channelled into narrow and restricted concepts, nor do we mean that they should be taught that there is any one particular way of drawing or painting, or indeed of making a three-dimensional figure. We would rather they be given paint, pencil, clay or even plasticine and asked to experiment with these, than be restricted to one person's ideas of what is or is not art. However, if they are allowed to practise a variety of techniques, such as simple air-brushing with paint (using paint blown down a straw, or flicked from an old toothbrush), masking, various forms of shading, and even two or three-point perspective, then they will be more able to express their visual ideas to their own satisfaction. The authors have encouraged children to use all these techniques in the primary school, often in combination, albeit at the appropriate stage of their development.

The ultimate aim is for children to be skilled in the use of a range of artistic media and then combine two or more of these to produce the finished piece. The main role for the teacher is often to tell the children when to stop, rather than when to start, as they are always tempted to do too much.

Art in practice

Art should be a practical subject, and the majority of the time given over to it should be spent by the children actually producing a picture or an artefact. Many subjects require this 'hands-on' approach: Science without a practical element becomes nothing more than at best a string of facts and at worst simple mythology, and how can Music be taught without some instrumental or vocal involvement at some stage? Of course there are activities within even these subjects that can be purely intellectual – the so-called 'minds-on' activities (Watt, 1999). We have ourselves used these in the classroom, but we would argue that they can rarely take place without a sound understanding of these subjects. As these are essentially practical subjects this knowledge can only be fully understood through practical 'hands-on' activities.

One example of this approach is illustrated by the following project.

Box 3.1 Painting the Jackson Pollock way

Our thanks to Karen Smith and Ian Watson, together with the children of their respective classes at Kenningtons Primary School, Aveley, Thurrock, for this case study.

This project not only involved children from two classes of very different ages (Karen Smith's children were of Year 2, while Ian Watson's were a mixed Year 5 and 6 class), but also the caretaker, parents and at least one of the school's governors! This was very much a collaborative project. It had to be highly organized, with carefully planning by both of the teachers involved. Each had his or her own ideas and these were discussed and refined until a workable and practical solution evolved, which would allow all children to benefit, irrespective of their age and ability. By the time that the teachers and children were ready to start work, any possible

Figure 3.1 The children producing their Jackson Pollock picture

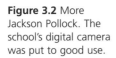

Figure 3.2 More Jackson Pollock. The school's digital camera was put to good use.

difficulties had been foreseen and allowed for, two trainee teachers had joined the project, and the youngest children had had more time to acquire some of the basic knowledge of this kind of painting, as well as an idea of how it could be done.

Although the idea of the topic had been discussed and planned for some time, it was the ICT unit from the QCA scheme of work 2B, in which the painting 'Yellow Islands' was described and illustrated, that provided the starting point. Karen Smith had shown this to her class who, young as they were, showed enthusiasm and interest in the processes and concepts involved in this kind of painting. Consequently both teachers collected various plastic spray bottles (the sort that kitchen cleaner comes in), washing-up liquid bottles, and a collection of old spoons and similar utensils.

In order not to use the best paint in the store, they then gathered all the odd tins of powder paint from around the school (we all have them if we are honest!). The children did not use paper for the paintings, but a strong, cream coloured fabric – a present from a governor. The object of the topic, together with details of how it was to be carried out, were explained in a letter home to all the parents, who were also asked to send in old clothes for their children to wear. Suitable clothing was found for those children whose parents did not respond. In some cases, bin bag dresses were used, which covered the youngest children from head to toe!

As the project was to be carried out in the school hall, albeit just before half-term when the floor was due to be resurfaced, the floor was covered with tarpaulins and plastic sheeting – hence the involvement of the school's caretaker. At lunchtime some of the older children helped to mix the powder paint. The fabric was then spread out on the floor covering. This fabric was about 5 feet wide, and various lengths were used, ranging from 6 to about 15 feet.

All the children were gathered in the hall, and after a short discussion in which they were reminded of Jackson Pollock and his paintings, and how they had been done and to some extent why, some of the children were invited to put some paint on the first piece of fabric, using at first the spoons to dribble the paint on, and afterwards the plastic containers to spray and squirt paint on. There followed another short discussion about the mixture of colours and their general effect, after which the children were separated into mixed age groups and let loose!

When the paintings were finished, the hall was cleared and the paintings left to dry over half-term. The completed paintings were heavy with the wet paint so needed the half-term holiday.

This was a carefully planned project carried out by all the children. It took place over two years ago, and those children still at the school, who are now in year 4, can remember it well.

ICT and art

We have already stated how important we think it is for children to actually use materials to paint, draw or model, and we hope that the above case study illustrates this very well. However, it is interesting to note that it originated from an idea derived from an ICT program, although no actual 'painting' took place on a screen, nor was this necessary. Does this mean that if they use one of the many programs available to produce a coloured picture they are not 'doing' Art? Yes, possibly, for it could be argued that this kind of activity is more in keeping with Design rather than Art. However, we have no desire to be pedantic – the subject is Art and Design after all. Moreover, there are art packages that allow the children to produce their own pictures based on the work of painters who seem to have a very mathematical approach to their art. We have described how programs that include painters such as Mondrian allow children to create their own pictures using a series of parallel lines and regular squares and rectangles, some of which can be coloured. This computer art need not be the finished object. It could instead be used as a basic design for a more ambitious painting or artefact, using a variety of appropriate materials.

There are many art programs available for the primary school. However, the teacher needs to make sure that these have an artistic input as well as an ICT one. If they just move ready-made pictures around the screen, then there may be little artistic merit involved, although such programs may motivate and encourage the children to develop their ideas. Two art programs that do more than this, in that they allow children, at different levels, to create designs using a variety of painting techniques and a choice of several shapes, colours, motifs, and backgrounds, are the Granada Learning (Black Cat) Fresco, and 2Simple's 2Paint.

Box 3.2   Self-portraits and finger puppets

Our thanks go to Rachel Hiley, a trainee teacher at Anglia Ruskin University.

The children were using 2paint to support a range of ongoing classroom activities. These included self portraits and pictures of finger puppets that they had made. Some of these are illustrated below.

Figure 3.3 A self portrait by Craig.

Figure 3.4 A finger puppet design.

Figure 3.5 A child's illustration of their finger puppet.

Using the Internet to support art

One other important use for the computer in an Art or Design project is to search the Internet for examples of the work of any given artist. Most of the world's major museums and art galleries have excellent websites that have online electronic versions of their collections. Although there are of course copyright considerations involved here, an email to the museum or gallery concerned to ask for permission to copy images will usually bring an affirmative response. The pupils and teachers can then copy or download paintings for use in their classrooms, either as part of their studies or as a teaching and learning aid. The picture can be copied and pasted onto a PowerPoint slide and printed out. It can even be laminated for future use – a set of instant pictures!

This is an excellent resource when studying the work of a particular artist or genre of artists. For example, if the children are studying Impressionist paintings, there will of course be prints of some of them in the classroom. In the above case study for example, now that they are older, the children could find more about Jackson Pollock and similar artists, and perhaps discover some of the reasons for painting in this way. They might find some of it difficult to understand – many adults do – but it will at least open their minds to new and interesting ideas. However, using the Web not only makes available a greater range of examples, it will give background information of the painters themselves, and make the children aware that art is not just a parochial activity, but is of world-wide interest and significance.

Using digital technologies to enhance art and design

The use of digital technologies, especially scanners and digital cameras, can significantly enhance the use of ICT in Art and Design. Quite apart from being excellent resources in their own right (as illustrated in the Jackson Pollock), when they are combined with or extended by the use of a graphics or an image manipulation package, some extremely powerful outcomes can result.

Although designed to scan text documents or images such as drawings, paintings or photographs, with a little imagination, a scanner can be a creative tool in its own right. Working in a similar manner to a colour photocopier, but connected directly to a computer, an image is scanned into a computer via the scanner, and is then saved. This can be done either through software that is supplied with the scanner or through an option as part of an application, usually in the 'insert' menu. A vast range of applications allow this: even Microsoft Word has an option to allow inserting an image onto a page directly from a scanner or digital camera. This provides additional flexibility as a document or image can be scanned and placed straight into another application for immediate use.

The scanner is increasingly becoming a tool to extend existing work or even to create new work 'from scratch'. For example, an artist may place an object or objects into a scanner and then begin the scan. Moving the object 'mid-scan' can produce some very effective and original work, characterized by merging colours and lines, and spiralling and swirling effects. Likewise, artwork produced by more traditional means, such as a charcoal or pencil drawing, can be scanned and subsequently manipulated through the use of a graphics package to create new artwork. Images can also be captured using a digital camera – still or video – which can then be downloaded to a computer using a direct USB connection.

Whether using a digital camera or a scanner, or even an image copied or downloaded from the Internet, the result is the same – an image that is saved on the computer as a digitized, electronic file. This is an important concept to understand, for in order for this type of work to be at its most effective, it should be appreciated that a new approach to these 'traditional' art forms is being used. As with all ICT, the most effective use is not always simply to use traditional and existing techniques on electronic media. These existing techniques are vital in themselves. ICT is at its best when an entirely new approach is utilized – an approach that would not be possible without the use of ICT.

The key point here is that this now represents the beginning of the process, not the end, as would be the case with more traditional means of image capture. For example, when using a film camera, the image would be captured (what used to be referred to as 'taking the photograph'), but could not be viewed until the film had been finished, removed from the camera and developed and printed. This was a complete process that for most people using commercial photographic developers could take several days (or weeks even, if one was slow at taking photographs!). Digital technology allows immediacy with a huge range of flexibility. In the same way that text can be manipulated by a word processor, so an image can be reprocessed in an infinite number of ways. And as we have already seen, any information on a computer is provisional, so it can be altered and reprocessed many times. If the artist is not happy with the result, then it can be discarded immediately, or indeed at any stage of the process. This can be at the point of capture by a scanner or digital camera or when subsequently saved much later as a file within another application (such as a word processor or graphics package). It is this provisionality that provides the key opportunities for ICT in art and design.

Box 3.3   Producing an interactive presentation using Microsoft PowerPoint for the history of art

A good illustration of the range and scope of the possibilities is an Art and Design ICT activity undertaken by one of the authors with his primary trainee teachers at Anglia Ruskin University. The trainees were set the challenge of producing an interactive Microsoft PowerPoint presentation that included a final total of six images – three 'originals' and three reprocessed. This could have two outcomes. At the simplest level it is a teaching aid, containing a series of images collected from a range of sources; or at a more complex level, it could be used as an interactive, clickable presentation, with the original images hyperlinking elsewhere. This could be a reprocessed or manipulated version of the original, a close-up detail of the original or something completely different, such as an external website.

The three original images were collected from separate sources: for example, one from a digital camera, one from a scanner and one from the Web. The image captured from the digital camera could be anything – an individual, an object or perhaps a view. The scanned image could be from a book, newspaper or indeed any other source. As detailed above, this could also include scans of original artwork produced away from the computer, such as paintings or drawings, or could even be work produced by the scanner itself. The third image, collected from the Web, was usually a painting from one of the many excellent museum or gallery websites. These original resources were saved in a specially created folder on the computer, which was easy to locate and access. (File management is important here, as it is important to keep the originals in case the subsequent reprocessed results are not what are ultimately required.)

These original images were then reprocessed in an image manipulation package such as Jasc Paint Shop Pro 8 or the more basic Microsoft Photo Editor. These may perhaps be complicated for primary school use, but this could also be done with many of the easier-to-use primary school packages that contain similar image manipulation tools. These include the paintbrush, drawing, cropping and effects tools. The first two are fairly self-explanatory, and when used carefully and used imaginatively, can add a great deal to an image. In fact, it is the effect tools that are probably the most useful – and certainly the most appealing to primary-aged children. There is a range of literally dozens of effects that can be utilized, either separately or in combination, to change the images in an infinite number of ways. These include a range of 3D effects, such as bevelling (raising) and chiselling (lowering); adding artistic effects such as charcoal, brushstrokes or pencil; a whole range of effects such as neon glowing or sepia toning; distortion effects such as spiky or swirling; geometric effects such as creating circular or cylindrical effects; illumination effects; and texture or reflection effects. This is in addition to other, more basic functions such as the ability to flip, mirror or rotate the image.

Once the artist was happy with the results, the new images were then saved with file names that were different from the originals, so that these were not overwritten in case they were needed again – perhaps to form the basis of further new work, or to be reused if the artist was unhappy with the subsequent outcome.

Once this was done, the images could then be inserted into a PowerPoint presentation and used in a number of ways. This software is ideal for displaying images, preferably one image per slide. For example, if the teacher was looking at the work of a particular artist for an art history project, different pictures of that artist's work could be inserted onto separate slides and presented to the class. If the teacher wished to examine a particular aspect of a painting (such as perspective), or a particular detail, he or she could crop the picture until only the required area of the picture remained. The remaining image could then be stretched out so that it was enlarged over the whole slide. The slides could then be viewed as a linear presentation, or be hyperlinked through the use of action buttons or 'hot spots'. The originals and reprocessed images could also be linked in this way.

How to hyperlink slides in Microsoft PowerPoint

Open Microsoft PowerPoint and select 'Blank Presentation' from the 'New' section of the menu on the righthand side of the screen; and then select the 'Blank Screen' option from the 'Content Layouts' menu on the righthand side of the screen. Go to the 'Insert' menu and select 'Picture from File' option. (This is why it is important to collect all of your resources to a separate folder on your own computer first, so that they are easy to find and access for situations such as this.)

In this case, the file called 'Water Lillies.jpg' has been selected, which is one of the images located by default in the 'My Pictures' folder that is supplied with Windows XP. At this point, users will need to select their own images. The image will fill the slide. If it is a smaller image, the user will need to use the handles located in each corner of the image to drag it out to fill the slide.

A second image needs to be inserted onto a new slide. This will be the image that the first slide links to. The 'Picture' tool bar needs to be displayed through selection from the 'View' menu, as this contains the tools that will enable the image to be edited. This is a 'floating' toolbar, which means that it can be moved round the screen. Using the 'Crop' tool shown on the tool bar, the edges of the image are removed, leaving the required detail, in this case one of the flowers. Click this again to turn the 'Crop' tool off.

Using the handles, the image can be stretched out to fill the slide. The two slides are then ready to be linked together. This can be done in three ways. The first, and most obvious, is to treat it as a linear slideshow and just click on the slide. However, the most interesting presentations are those that use hyperlinks through 'action buttons' or 'hot spots'.

Creating action buttons

Select the 'Action Buttons' option from the 'Slide Show' menu. Then choose the appropriate button. The cursor will change into a cross-hair. Move it to the desired position and drag out to the required size. A new window will appear with an option to link the button to the required slide. Choose the required option from the drop-down list, and then select 'OK'. However, always remember to uncheck the boxes under 'Advance Slide' on the menu on the righthand slide of the screen, otherwise the presentation will continue to advance in a linear manner.

Creating hot spots

A more interesting and imaginative way is to create a series of 'hot spots' in the image, whereby pointing and clicking certain parts of the image takes the user through to another image, or perhaps a zoomed part of the original. These are very common on websites and multimedia CD-Roms – especially those of art galleries and museums – and are very easy to make.

Find the appropriate image and paste it into a PowerPoint slide. Using the 'Draw' tools, which can be found just below the picture, choose a shape and use it to cover the area of the original that you want to be the hyperlinked hot spot. Then right click on the shape and select 'Hyperlink' from the bottom of the menu. Then follow the same process as detailed for the 'action buttons'.

Using the 'Fill' and 'Line' tools, again situated just below the picture, click on the drop down arrows and remove the colour shading and the line so that the shape is invisible, using the 'No Fill' and 'No Line' options. You now have an invisible shape, acting as a layer above the image, which acts as the hyperlinked hot spot. When the presentation is run as a slide show, clicking here will move to the required slide. This will be indicated by the cursor turning into a hand when moved across the active area.

This is a simple yet effective way of presenting art work, and can be completed either by the teacher for display, or simply as a teaching resource. Pupils can use it as a means of displaying their own work. It does not necessarily require expensive, specialist software (although this can be used if wished), yet still provides many rewarding and challenging results. Quite apart from the artistic input, a range of simple ICT skills are also taught, which provides an excellent example of how ICT capability can be developed.

An effective alternative or extension activity is to use a digital video camera. The pupils can make a film, which when edited using software such as Pinnacle Studio, can have various effects added. This particular program has four effects: blur, emboss, mosaic and posterize. Either a 'moving' special effects film can be created, or individual screens can be grabbed and used in the same way as the examples identified above. (Digital video will be discussed in greater depth in the chapter on Physical Education.)

Design

If children are to use Design in the context of this subject, then teachers need to decide if their pupils are going to base the designs on a future painting or are they going to be drawings that will stand alone as pictures in their own right. In this latter case they may represent the presentational drawings mentioned in the chapter on Design and Technology. There we suggested that the designs should be ideas and later plans for an actual working model or artefact. However, if the designed product was part of a marketing project, then final drawings might be needed to help display and sell what had been made: in short, acting as an advertisement. In the primary school these drawings need not be complex. A simple Food Technology project based on any cookery-based lesson, or the packaging of some simple bathroom cosmetic, previously bought in bulk for the school's summer fete, can be treated in this way. Making drawings of their various ideas for packaging the product, and final presentational drawings, are all part of this kind of project.

Art and design across the curriculum

The authors have found that through Art children can be motivated to take a fresh look at other areas of the curriculum. We have already suggested how Art can be used in the teaching of Mathematics (Williams and Easingwood, 2004). One example involved the drawing of mathematical nets, and their subsequent use as mini-sculptures. The ICT net-drawing activity described in Chapter 2 would be relevant here. Projects for both History and Science can also be art-based. Not only is there an intrinsic historical element in all but the most recent paintings, many painters used science and technology as a source of inspiration. Joseph Wright of Derby (1734–1797) is an obvious example, as is Adolph Menzel (1815–1905). Both these artists painted scenes of metal workers in factories and foundries, although Wright is also famous for his paintings of scientific experiments set in a contemporary social context. However, a painting does not need to illustrate a specific science activity.

Many paintings can include subjects that can be used to motivate children in a Science project, or indeed other subjects such as History, Geography or Mathematics. These could be paintings of railways, building sites, or even clocks and mirrors (Field and James, 1997). The children should be encouraged to find such artists, together with examples of their work, on the Web.

Design skills and art

The children will need to learn some basic design skills. These may be more necessary for Design than they are for Art, although of course many artists are very often highly skilled draughtsmen and women. It is perhaps that there can be 'rules' attached to Design, because it may be perceived to have a more functional use than Art, which is more spontaneous, although in different ways of course just as important. Even if the children are making a simple design that will form the basis of a later painting – perhaps for a still life or a landscape – they will still need drawing skills if they are to do more than just an outline.

However, at this stage we need to make sure that we do not overemphasize the need for these 'pre-painting designs'. Some painters do draw outlines before putting paint to canvas. They may even sketch in the details of a landscape on the canvas, take photographs and write notes about what they see, before returning to their studio to finish the painting. There are as many others however who do no such thing, and will paint the picture in situ or even rely entirely on their memory to produce it some time later. These methods are as individual as the artists concerned, and will obviously result in very different paintings even of the same subject. Surely this is what we should expect from a class of 30 or so children. If we insist that children make a design for a painting, then we may restrict their imagination and run the risk of losing all spontaneity.

The elements of design

These are traditionally, line, shape, size, colour, value, direction, and texture. Obviously these can apply to almost any picture, be it a drawing or painting, perhaps even a photograph: but for design work these can be more precise, and even on occasion proscribed.

Line

To a large extent this is self-explanatory, in that it refers to the continuous mark made by the pencil, pen or brush that delineates the object to be portrayed. More precisely it refers to the other elements used by the designer or artist to lead the viewer's eye through the picture. In commercial art and design it can specifically refer to stark black and white drawings, using only hatching to achieve shades of grey.

Shape

This is not only the form that the subject takes, but its configuration within the picture. To some extent in a design this is often governed by the necessity to portray the object to its best advantage.

Colour

Not as obvious as it seems, as a designer will need to pay particular attention to which colour will give the correct visual impression, and therefore which colour medium to use to obtain the required effect. This could be oil or acrylic paint, coloured pencil, marker pen, or, as is often the case with design, gouache – a high quality, opaque water paint.

Value

This refers to the range of colour from light to dark, and is based on a ten-point scale. Although it can depend on which scale you use, generally high values tend to be light and low values dark. While any colour can be graded in this way, in design it is particularly relevant to the gradation of black through various shades of grey to white.

Direction

This refers to the movement of the viewer's eye through a picture. This is very important in design, and the so called 'eye path' is carefully created by the calculated use of the other elements.

Texture

This is the representation of a surface of the object drawn, which could be anything from rough, even jagged, to (more usually in design) smooth and reflective.

Teaching these elements

Teachers will need to decide just how much of this can be taught to primary age children. In the experience of the authors this is a surprising amount, at least where the older children are concerned. Line, shape and colour are fairly basic requirements in any picture, and when explained to them, we have often found that children are very interested to find that paintings are not always put together in any haphazard way. This does not restrict their imagination: indeed, we have found that to the contrary, they are often motivated to experiment and create more interesting pictures. In the case of 'strict' design their pictures may anyway be circumscribed by other requirements.

Box 3.4   An activity to illustrate the concept of value and texture

Value

Children seem to have little difficulty in understanding this concept. Give them a long piece of paper and two colours, perhaps black and white, although any other colour can be used along with white. Paint a thick line of 'pure' colour at the top, and then add a given amount of white to a second line beneath this. Repeat this for seven more lines down the page, one under the other, doubling the amount of white each time – perhaps using one dip of the brush, then two dips, three dips and so on. A tenth line of pure white will complete the exercise. Obviously some practice is needed to obtain an even gradation of colour, but this is a practical 'hands-on' experience and one which will help children when it comes to painting a 'real' picture.

As an additional cross-curricular activity the teacher can ask them to think of one 'feeling-type word' to describe some of the colours that they make. Bright red could perhaps suggest fear or a loud noise such as a shriek, another colour a whisper. Greens might represent calmness or peace, while light blues and white are of course traditionally cold colours. It is not difficult to imagine what they would make of black, but grey should be interesting. Thinking about colours in this way will help them to decide which to use for any particular kind of subject they have it in mind to paint.

Texture

There are many paintings that depend as much on this as on the medium used. The thickness of the paint may be all that is needed, but young children can create many different textures on paper or card to suit the subject. It is an interesting skill and one which will give them not only much pleasure but will allow them yet more scope to produce a range of interesting pictures.

Simply mixing various different substances such as sand and glue with the paint will give an interesting textured effect. Indeed, the rougher the texture required the easier it seems to be. To obtain a really smooth and reflective finish is much more difficult. For this children will probably need to have had some experience of pencil drawing, experimenting with light and shade. It will help if they have been introduced to 'value' as described above, for they can then experiment with different shades of paint, as well as pure white, to see what effects they can achieve.

ICT and design

If we accept that design is at least to some extent functional, then using a good program to aid design is not only a valuable tool in its own right, but will help to motivate children to begin to learn these basic skills. Like any other subject, to some these will come more quickly than to others, and an imaginative teacher will use a wide variety of aids to accomplish this.

The skilful use of ICT is one such aid. There are some very good programs available made specifically for the primary school. One such program is Black Cat's Designer. This can be used by both Key Stage 1 and 2, and allows children to draw freehand as well as to use ready-programmed shapes. It also enables them to alter their designs, as well as to rotate and flip them. Again, these kinds of activities do not necessarily need specialist software, as Microsoft's Word and PowerPoint have some useful drawing tool functions, as does the software that comes with most interactive whiteboards. This is illustrated later in the section about fabric designs.

Box 3.5 Simple perspective drawings

Teachers can also use the computer's own design programs, such as Microsoft Draw. The two examples of this program shown here illustrate how children can use this to make simple perspective drawings.

In Figure 3.6, the front vertical edge is drawn first. Two points left and right of this are chosen as the 'vanishing point' for the two lines that are drawn from the top and bottom of the vertical line. After these are drawn, two more vertical lines are drawn to mark the other edges of the shape. The final lines are drawn from the top of each vertical line to the respective vanishing points. It will depend on what view of the cube is required as to where these are situated. Move them down below the base of the cube and you will get a 'worm's eye view' of the shape.

Note that all lines other than vertical must follow the lines to the 'vanishing point'. For perspective, in Figure 3.7 wheels are drawn as ovals and not circles. The front 'cuboid' section of the van can be left as a blunt windscreen, or it can be deleted to give the more common bonnet and windscreen. The windscreen would be drawn in using the lefthand vanishing point.

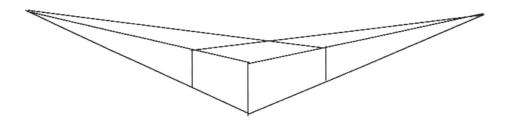

Figure 3.6 Two point perspective drawn using the Microsoft Word drawing tools.

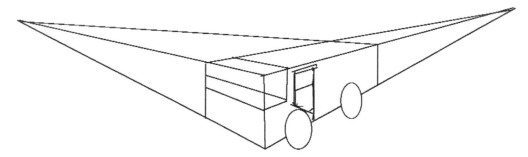

Figure 3.7 Using the cuboid perspective drawing to draw a van, again with the Microsoft Word drawing tools.

It should be understood that although many programs allow similar cuboid shapes to be shown on the screen, these will mostly be mathematically correct shapes, which are not drawn in perspective. Such 'artistic' shapes will often have to be done by hand, be it on paper, or on the screen using a specific drawing program. A useful way of doing this is to use the 'AutoShapes' tool, which is part of both Microsoft's Word and PowerPoint programs. By using these in conjunction with the '3-D Style' button, a series of shapes that appear to be three-dimensional can be created, and then dragged or rotated around the screen in a huge number of permutations. They can also be 'Illuminated' to give different senses of perspective. When all of this is done on an interactive whiteboard, either by the teacher or the pupils, the results can be very impressive indeed, and can assist the teaching of the concept of perspective. Some examples of this are illustrated below.

• Begin with a 5x5 square drawn on the slide.

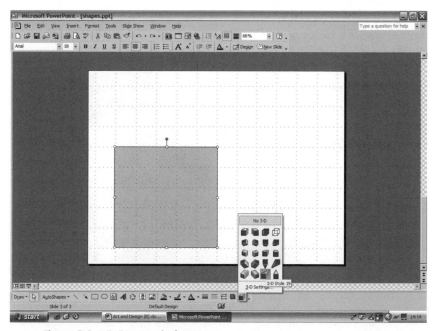

Figure 3.8 A 5×5 square is drawn

• The '3D Settings' shape tool menu is then selected.

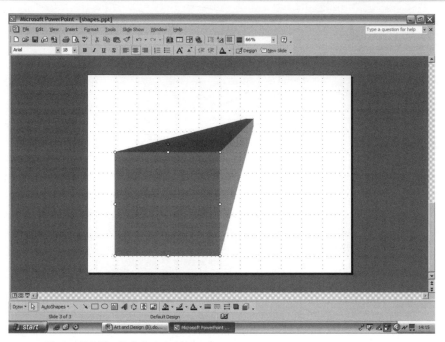

Figure 3.9 The 'Infinity' option

• In this case, the 'Infinity' option is selected.

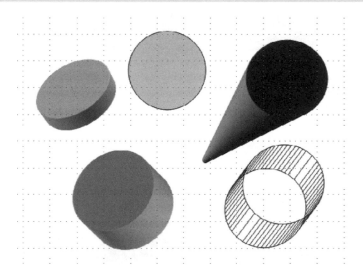

Figure 3.10 A range of 3-D shapes created in Microsoft PowerPoint, which originated with a two dimensional circle (top). By using the '3-D settings', a range of different perspectives and positions can be used. To rotate a shape, click on the required shape and drag the green handle.

An interesting aspect of these examples is the shading that helps to give the shapes solidity and depth. If it is a simple cuboid that is being drawn, the designer will need to decide from which direction the light will come. For example, if the view of the shape shows its front, top and the righthand side, with the light shining on it from above and behind but slightly to the left, then the shading will need to show this. Hence the front of the shape will be the side most shaded, and the right side slightly less. The top, which has the light shining almost directly on it, will need very little shading at all. In practical terms this could mean that the front has three layers of colour, the right side two and the top one. In addition, the top together with the front right hand edge could be highlighted with a little white to suggest some reflection.

As helpful as they are, it is nevertheless important to realize that using these shapes alone does not in itself teach drawing. They may help to set a 'picture' of depth in the mind of the user, and to some extent show how light and shade can be used to suggest a three-dimensional solid (in the way we have described). However, the point of learning to draw such shapes and how to shade them to give a sense of solidity is that they form the basis of all natural objects. A human shape can first be drawn as a series of spheres and cylinders, or a car may start out as a cube with ellipse (oval) shaped wheels, as the van did in Figure 3.7. This illustrates how simple line diagrams can be drawn on a blank screen, just in the way that they can on a plain piece of paper. The guidelines to the vanishing points are there simply to allow for the correct perspective to be drawn, and can be removed afterwards. Colour and shade can then be added, and as a final touch details such as van fittings or lettering and advertisements. These latter would of course be drawn in using the same perspective guide lines. Although Figure 3.7 is a typical blunt-nosed van shape, if we were drawing the most stream-lined sports car, it would begin as a cubic shape drawn to perspective. The curves of the car would be drawn within the shape so that it would keep proper three-dimensional perspective. In a similar way, details of the human face can be drawn within an ellipse, or even a complete head drawn within a sphere.

It is for these reasons that we feel it is essential that Art and Design remains essentially a practical subject, in which such things as line, shape, value, and texture, all described above, need to be understood. The best art programs allow for this in that users have to make their own decisions and apply them in a similar way to how they would if they were using paper and paint. The work is not all done for them and they have to take responsibility for the finished picture. In a similar way, a good design program should allow children to use line and shape to make their own plans or designs. By all means it should give them as much help as possible, as well as including 'extras' such as shapes, colours, pictures, or a choice of letters to enhance the finished drawing. However, if the child simply clicked on an icon to show a ready-drawn object, they would never learn to draw anything.

A design program that allows the user to really design an object is Design and Create, described in some detail in Chapter 2. Although produced for the more technological subjects, in its design mode it allows the user to make simple or intricate line drawings while still allowing for the use of colour, shading and depth, as well as offering a range of 'ready-made' pictures that can be used to enhance any final presentational drawing.

Textiles and ICT

Although working with textiles in the primary school may be limited to tie and dye, potato and leaf prints or simple stencils, there is still plenty of scope for children to experiment with both colour and texture. Tie and dye can be used in a Science project about colour (Williams, 1991), and it is in the Science part of this project that ICT could be used. Textiles using potato prints or cut-out stencils often have a regular pattern, reproduced many times on the material. This can be replicated on a computer screen, perhaps mimicking the work of Escher, a mathematician who explored the use of repeating similar shapes to produce new patterns. By using these programs children can see how their chosen pattern will look, and can adjust it in ways that will allow them to decide on a final design.

Imaginative use of some of the background scenes with Promethean's Activstudio software, which drives their Activboard, can further extend and enhance this idea, as illustrated below. The user begins by selecting a suitable background that readily lends itself to be transformed or rotated. In this example, the 'Flag' option from the tile backgrounds in the 'Fun' menu has been used.

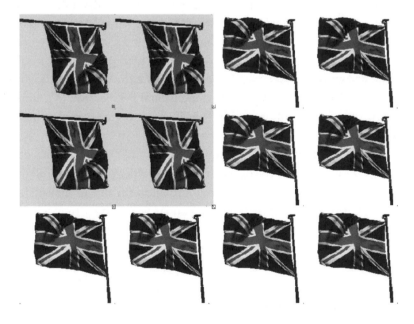

Figure 3.11 A larger area can also be selected. In this example four flags have been selected and transformed by being mirrored and then rotated through 90 degrees.

The 'camera' option from the main menu is then selected, and by clicking on the 'Area Snapshot' option, the user can 'photograph' a given area of the background by dragging the mouse over the required tiles, in this case one of the flags. The righthand mouse button is then clicked and the option 'To current flipchart page' selected. This opens a further menu that allows the user to transform the selected area in a number of ways, such as rotating a central flag through 180 degrees. This effect can also be achieved by using the 'Flip' or 'Mirror' options in the X or Y axes.

By using these programs children can obtain a preview of what their textile print could look like. It allows them to experiment with different shapes, many of which they can eventually use for the actual stencils, or which can at the very least help them decide which shape or pattern to use. As an interactive whiteboard is being used, this activity can form the basis of a whole class discussion.

Box 3.6 Using Microsoft Powerpoint to produce repeated and tessellated shapes as a prelude to fabric design

The image in Figure 3.12 was created by a right-angled triangle being selected from the 'AutoShapes' menu at the bottom of the screen. This was then 'rubber banded' into a 3x4 'rectangle' size and positioned as the top left triangle. This shape was then copied and pasted three times, with each subsequent shape being rotated through 90 degrees clockwise. This was done using the green dragging handle, which appears when the shape is highlighted. To assist with the placing of the shapes, the 'Grid and Guides' option was selected from the 'Draw' menu, and the 'Snap to grid' option switched on. The size of the grid can be selected and changed, depending upon the size of the shapes required. In order to manipulate the shapes on the screen, PowerPoint needs to be used in edit mode, rather than slide show mode. The image above looks very similar to what it might look like if it had been used with software supplied with an interactive whiteboard, such as the Promethean Activstudio, which is supplied with the Promethean Activboard.

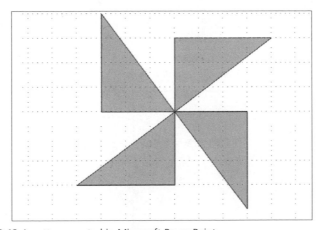

Figure 3.12 A pattern created in Microsoft PowerPoint.

This particular point would act as a good starting point for work involving tessellations, where the same shape is repeated a number of times and is then fitted together on the screen. This can be achieved simply by using tools that are included as part of the software for producing a range of regular shapes, and can be filled with colour from the paint tools. By copying and pasting, the child is able to experiment on the screen to discover which shapes will tessellate. This provides the opportunity to fully explore the properties of a range of shapes, while becoming familiar with the important functions of the software, which in turn will allow further experimentation at a more advanced level. Although there is no substitute for children fitting 'real' shapes made of cardboard or plastic together, the use of ICT enables the child to produce patterns quickly, easily, neatly, accurately and consistently, all crucially important when exploring the properties of space and shape.

For example, repeated tessellated patterns can be drawn in Microsoft PowerPoint. These can be produced by copying the original right-angled triangle seven times, and dragging them into position. The gaps are filled by copying the shaded triangles, rotating them through 180 degrees and using the 'No fill' option to remove the shading.

Drawing shapes on a computer also allows the development of several key ICT skills, which can be subsequently used in a range of contexts. The most obvious of these are the skills to use the 'Cut', 'Copy' and 'Paste' tools, which when used in conjunction with 'Rotation' tools, for example, can be used to create some fairly sophisticated transformations. 'Rotation' tools allow the required shape to be rotated through a given number of degrees: usually 45 or 90 degrees, but more advanced packages allow rotation through any number of degrees. However, especially with younger children, there is little need to use any other measurement as this may become confusing for the child – the notion of turning a shape the equivalent of a right angle or half a right angle is much easier to comprehend. The key teaching point here is that shapes can be moved into any position without any of the properties changing.

Other useful tools include 'Mirror' tools, which as the name suggests, allow the mirroring of shapes along the X or Y axes and are especially useful for symmetry. When used with the 'Rotate' tool, this can be developed into rotational symmetry, particularly useful when teaching this as part of the Key Stage 2 Mathematics curriculum. The 'Flip' tool performs a similar function, allowing shapes to be 'flipped' in the X or Y axis. This is illustrated by Figure 3.13 below.

In Figure 3.13, the right-angled triangles have been rotated and moved into new positions using the 'Rotate' or 'Flip' tools in the 'Draw' menu. This is quite a complex skill which develops a range of ICT skills and logical thinking. The shapes have been rotated using the 'Flip Horizontal' and 'Flip Vertical' tools. Other shapes can be 'made', for example the triangles can be rotated 90 degrees clockwise and rearranged into a tessellating pattern.

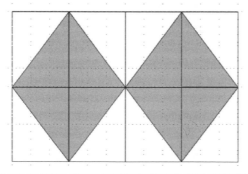

Figure 3.13 A tessellating pattern produced in Microsoft PowerPoint.

When these functions are completed on an interactive whiteboard, either by the teacher or by pupils, the results can be very impressive indeed. The shapes can be manipulated in a number of different ways quickly and easily. This dynamic environment allows the children to see how the properties of individual shapes can be altered – for example, by turning an equilateral triangle into an isosceles triangle – or even transformed into a completely different shape. This process is a kind of electronic version of the pegboard that is found in most Key Stage 1 classrooms, and this is also why this process is often known as 'rubber banding', as the edges and vertices of the shapes are dragged into different positions. This is a powerful learning tool: during a class lesson, everybody can see clearly what is going on, and can actively participate in the lesson. An example of this is illustrated by Figures 3.14 and 3.15.

Although effective, Figure 3.14 needs a great deal of care to create. In order to get a regular hexagon, it is necessary to hold the shift key down while dragging out the original shape. This ensures that equal edges and vertices are maintained, so that each subsequent copy will tessellate. When fitting the hexagons together, the 'Snap to grid' option should be turned off, otherwise they will not tessellate properly.

Figure 3.15 again started as a shape selected from the 'Basic Shapes' option in the 'AutoShapes' menu. The shift key is held down while the shape is dragged out to ensure that all edges and angles remain equal. The small yellow dot is the key handle here: when this is moved the shape is transformed, producing a new triangle. The original equilateral triangle can even be transformed into a right-angled triangle.

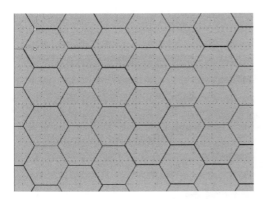

Figure 3.14 Hexagons tessellating.

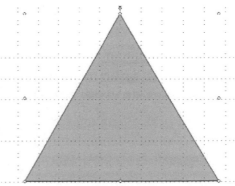

Figure 3.15 An equilateral triangle.

Box 3.7 Using an animated art and design program

ICT is most effectively used in any curriculum area when technology enables the child or the teacher to create in ways that would otherwise not be possible. This chapter has illustrated how the use of digital technologies such as cameras and scanners has extended the kind of Art and Design work that can be undertaken in primary classrooms. Although some extremely creative results can be attained using an art package, we should also look for a program that offers more than just static pictures: and this is now possible through the use of a simple yet effective animation package.

This program is 2Animate from 2Simple software. There is a choice of two levels, depending on the age and experience of the children, who can draw a series of up to five pictures, which are shown on a strip at the top of the screen. At a touch of an icon these pictures reproduce themselves in sequence. They could tell a simple story, or be used to illustrate the germination of a seed or the hatching of an egg (see Figures 3.16–3.20).

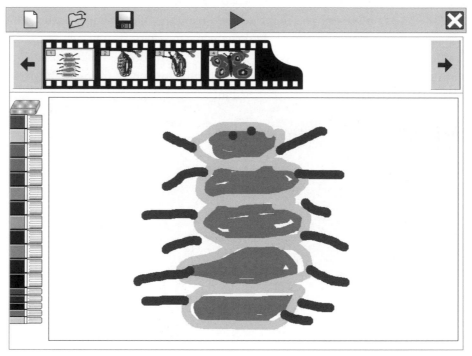

Figure 3.16 2Animate, from 2Simple software. This is 'Simple mode', which is designed for use by younger children. The drawings are created, and when the artist is satisfied that the frame is complete, clicks on the next frame and draws the next image in the sequence. This particular animation, a sample file called 'Butterfly', comes with the program, and shows a caterpillar metamorphosing into a butterfly. This is frame one.

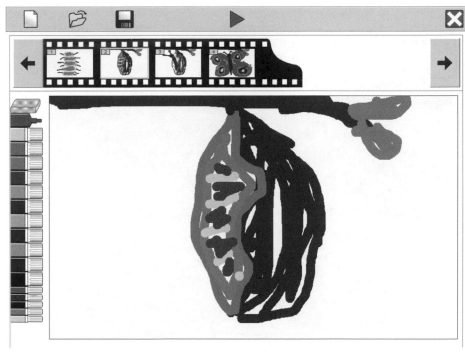

Figure 3.17 This is frame two, where the caterpillar turns into a chrysalis

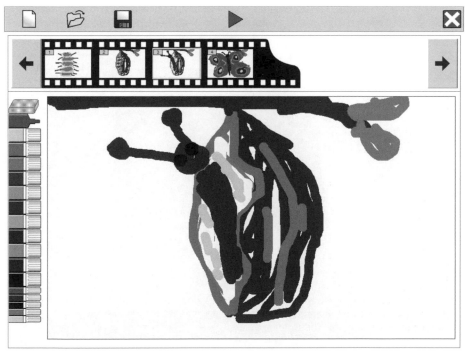

Figure 3.18 This is frame three, where the butterfly emerges from the chrysalis

Figure 3.19 This is frame four, where the butterfly flies away.

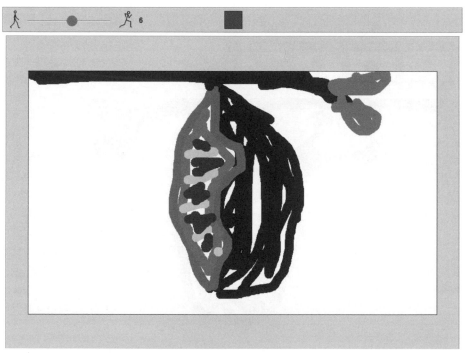

Figure 3.20 The speed of the animation can be set by using the slider bar at the top of the screen – towards the left slower, towards the right faster. This screen is accessed by clicking on the green arrow at the top of the preceding screen.

Advanced mode, which can be used by older children in Key Stages 1 and 2, contains some very useful features. Perhaps the most useful is the 'inbetweening' option, which allows the user to draw the first and last frames, and the computer then draws the intervening frames. For example, it might allow a stick man to be drawn, appearing to get closer and larger as the sequence runs.

On the 'Advanced Mode' screen mode, designs can be drawn that will be made one at a time on the large white rectangle and can then be reproduced on the 'film strip' above. These can then be activated to give an animated moving sequence.

There are other options. For example, by using a webcam 'real' pictures can be shown. These can be left as they are or be enhanced with superimposed drawings. This simple form of animation also allows children to explore how things move, particularly as the program also has the facility to deconstruct each picture so that the viewer can see how the image is formed.

Box 3.8   A newsletter

When computers first appeared in schools, they were often used as a word processor to produce a class or school newspaper. It was an exciting and innovative experience at the time to observe three or four children clustered round the screen in actual discussion about not only the content of the paper, but also its format and lay-out. While this may still be the case today (although it has to be said that neither of the authors has seen much evidence to suggest it is), perhaps by introducing the animated strip described above, the class or school newsletter could be given a new lease of life. For example, webcam pictures could show five shots of the school football team in action, together with some still pictures from the school digital camera. The complete newspaper could be put on disc for all to see.

ICT in support of art and design

Although by no means exhaustive, this chapter will hopefully have illustrated how the teaching and learning of Art and Design can be significantly enhanced by a range of uses of ICT, often without the need for specialist hardware and software. By employing the drawing and painting tools of industry-standard software such as Microsoft Office, or the software supplied with an interactive whiteboard such as Activstudio, simple yet effective results can be quickly and easily achieved. Even with a small outlay, cheap digital cameras and scanners can be purchased, and these can have a significant impact upon the teaching of Art and Design. When specialist software is utilized, some very impressive results indeed can be achieved.

When we talk about being creative with ICT, we do not always mean it in the literal sense; we often mean using it imaginatively to support a range of subjects in the curriculum. However, in the case of this particular subject, both aspects of creativity are easily achieved, with results that are instantly impressive. With a colour printer, teachers and pupils can create and produce effective artwork simply and quickly – although indeed, when using presentation software there isn't even a need to print out work. Many artists who use ICT as a means of creating and displaying their work often only use the screen, as it gives much better colour and resolution than the most expensive colour printer. However ICT is deployed, supporting Art and Design produces one of the most visually striking ways of using it in the primary school classroom.

References

DfEE/QCA. (1999) *The National Curriculum for England.* HMSO, London.

Field, J.V. and James, F.A.J.L. (1997) *Science in Art: Works in the National Gallery that illustrate History of Science and Technology*, Monograph No. 11. British Society for the History of Science.

Watt, D. (1997) 'Science: learning to explain how the world works', in J. Riley and R. Prentice (eds) *The Curriculum for 7-11 Year Olds.* Paul Chapman Publishers, London.

Williams, J. (1991) *Starting Technology – Colour and Light.* Wayland, Hove.

Williams, J. and Easingwood, N. (2004) *ICT and Primary Mathematics – A Teacher's Guide.* RoutledgeFalmer, London.

CD-Roms, programs and useful addresses

Technology Teaching Systems (TTS), Nunn Brook Road, Huthwaite, Sutton-in-Ashfield, Nottinghamshire, NG17 2HU – for technological equipment, and various kits, books, artefacts, games, musical instruments etc., for not only Science and Technology, but for many other subjects, such as History, Geography, Music, RE and Art. Also supplies a lot of software, including Black Cat's Designer and the Focus Educational Software's Design and Create program.

2Simple Software, Enterprise House, 2 The Crest, Hendon, London, NW4 2HN – for many valuable programs including 2Paint, 2Create – A Story, and 2Animate.

Granada Learning Ltd (including Black Cat Software), Granada Television, Quay Street, Manchester, M60 9EA – for various CD-Roms, interactive and simulation programs, and 'Black Cat' databases and spreadsheets.

Geography

Geography in the primary curriculum

Of all the subjects in the primary curriculum that have been squeezed out by the shift in emphasis towards literacy and numeracy in the last 20 years or so, Geography is the one that has perhaps suffered the most. Often subsumed into 'Humanities', or even removed from the curriculum altogether, despite the fact that it has a National Curriculum entitlement, this particular Foundation Subject has all but disappeared as a subject in its own right in some primary schools. Yet paradoxically, this is probably the one subject that can genuinely deliver and reinforce all that is good about what has traditionally been seen as good primary practice. The opportunities that Geography offers in terms of collaborative learning, first-hand experience, opportunities for enquiry-based learning and the corresponding development of investigative techniques, as well as the different areas of study that compose the wider subject of Geography, ensure that it should be a staple of the primary curriculum. The study of 'sub-subjects' such as mapwork, geology, geomorphology, meteorology, and human and social geography both at home and abroad, can be seen quite legitimately as subjects in their own right, and as such provide natural links to other areas of the curriculum such as Science (especially Biology, Environmental Science and Physics), Mathematics, Modern Foreign Languages and History. It is these elements and links that also provide excellent opportunities for the use of ICT. This chapter will explore how exploiting the power and potential of ICT can extend and enhance teaching and learning in all aspects of Geography – and not necessarily just using the rather obvious geographical resource of the Internet.

There are so many different aspects to this subject that it can be difficult to know where to begin. In some ways this is a similar problem to the one we describe later in the History chapter. In that case it is deciding where to start in time: but with Geography it is what part of the subject to teach, and whether one aspect is more important than another.

To a great extent what is taught depends on the time and resources available, and even the National Curriculum for England, which tells English schools what they must teach, has to allow for this. It is here as in most other subjects that the use of ICT is so valuable, although we must never think of it solely as a time-saving device. When used properly it does indeed save class time, which can be utilised for other activities that may themselves include other aspects of ICT. However, as we shall describe later, there are many examples of using ICT in ways which not only enhance the teaching of geography, but make it possible to include new and exciting aspects of the subject. The use of data-logging hardware and software, and the use of geographical information systems software with mapwork, can genuinely bring something to Geography that would be difficult to replicate by more 'traditional' means.

Having said this, we should also remember that what we teach must be appropriate for the age and ability of the individual child. Geography is essentially a practical subject, and as such observation and research must precede any abstract theory outside the experience of the primary school child. This is not to suggest that we teach them only the geography of their front doorstep. It does however mean that we should create imaginative and interesting ways of bringing the outside world into their immediate experience. We shall suggest ways of doing this later in the chapter, but we should first decide which aspects of Geography are appropriate for the primary school.

The different areas of study within geography

There are so many different areas of study within Geography that in Higher Education not only would a student eventually have to specialize in at least one of them, but there is often some argument over whether the subject is one of the Humanities, or should be included with the Sciences. It is often of course a link between the two, which in the opinion of the authors is one of its main strengths: and indeed it is difficult to see how in schools it can not form part of any cross-curricular activity, seeing how it so often involves History, Mathematics, Science and even Design and Technology. These observations need not (except the cross-curricular one) involve children in the primary school, although teachers should perhaps keep them in mind when planning a lesson or topic, as the activity described below illustrates.

Box 4.1   Making a shaduf

This is in fact a Design and Technology activity, as described in Williams, 1997. However, it has many geographical and ICT connections, as well as illustrating cross-curricular applications.

A shaduf (one of several spellings) is a simple water-raising device still found in many countries in Africa and on the Indian sub-continent. It is based on the principle of the first-type lever with a central fulcrum (perhaps a forked tree) next to the well, a bucket hanging from one end and a weight (sack of stones?) as a balance at the other end. All the user has to do is add their weight at the 'dry' end in order to raise the bucket.

Children can easily make a model of a shaduf, either from natural materials or more sophisticated equipment. They could even use a construction kit. The geographical implications are self-evident. Where are they found? Why is this type of technology still used? What are the implications for water use, irrigation, and general water supply? The answers to these questions together with other connected information can of course be found by careful and relevant use of the Internet. This kind of topic also allows children to study aspects of world wide geography arising from their own classroom activities.

It is important to emphasize the cross-curricular nature of the subject; Geography has so many natural links to most of the other subjects of the curriculum, and these need to be reinforced. Children do not think in isolation; the images of all aspects of geography to which they are constantly subjected by media such as TV, films and the Internet should provide a starting point for the study of Geography. For the moment, let us think what this wide ranging subject involves.

Political Geography

This is hardly a subject that we would teach in detail to young children. However, the UK is a country within the European Union, and this will of course be referred to in any appropriate topic. This may simply be a reference to the euro currency (as we describe in Chapter 7), or the school may even have links with other schools within the EU. There are good opportunities to look at maps of the countries of Europe, with the interactive whiteboard, CD-Roms and the Internet being particularly useful resources here. For older children, it will be useful to look at older maps too, to examine the changes that occurred to national boundaries and, indeed, to individual countries post-1945 and post-1990, when significant changes occurred in the old Eastern Bloc area. It is also important to ensure that every classroom has a globe and a set of up-to-date atlases to reflect the modern political situation. These should be relatively cheap, so that they can be replaced whenever the political situation changes – which it does frequently in such a rapidly changing world.

Environmental Geography

By this we do not mean the highly specialized area of biogeography, but a more general study of types of vegetation such as woodland, forest, grassland, and desert, and how it is used or indeed abused. While this might begin on a local scale, it should also eventually involve the whole world environment, for surely we now know that we are all affected by environmental changes that can take place thousands of miles away. For this reason a study of weather and climate should also be a part of this topic. The use of electronic weather stations, which record all meteorological conditions such as temperature, precipitation (rainfall or snowfall), barometric (air) pressure, wind speed and direction, is an important part of this area of geography, which quite rightly can and should be seen as a subject in its own right. The cross-curricular links to Science and Mathematics are also important. Data-logging provides an important ICT element here, with the capability constantly and automatically to log environmental features such as temperature and light forming a crucial part of the role of ICT in supporting environmental geography. This is discussed in greater depth later in this chapter.

Economic Geography

At primary level, this will largely be confined to describing the main industries of a chosen country, together with their main imports and exports. For this children will need some knowledge of world geography, and obviously ICT will be a necessary part of this. The use of the Internet will be an important factor here, as this is one of the principal ways in which pupils can find out about distant lands, using a means that is instant and dynamic. It is also important to take the opportunity to reinforce positive images of foreign countries, and to dispel any preconceptions or stereotypical views. Tasks related to this might include designing a set of stamps to promote the cultural and economic advantages of a given country, using an art package. The pupils could find out information from the Internet, television or the media, and then design and produce their own stamps, using digital images to reinforce their points and ideas. To extend this activity, the children might also design holiday brochures in an application such as Microsoft Word or Publisher, to emphasize the positive features of a country.

Physical Geography

The study of the physical structure of an environment is one that even young children find fascinating. They may previously have taken such features as rivers, valleys and hills, and even flatlands and beaches very much for granted. However, once they begin to understand how these were formed, how much the underlying rock structure may have influenced this, and how they are even now undergoing change, albeit slowly, in our experience children are motivated to learn more about how their world was formed. The current landscape of Britain, for example, has been significantly modified over hundreds of millions of years at different times by the action of the sea, rivers, glaciations, at least four ice ages, volcanic action and climatic change. Although it has become a little bit of a geographical cliché to say this, the past is the key to the present, and children need to learn and to understand that the planet is a constantly changing, dynamic environment and that their home location would have looked very different several million years ago to how it looks now.

On some parts of the British coastline, storm and wave action are changing the appearance of the coast much more rapidly, with large areas of beach and cliff disappearing every winter. This is a very good example of weather and climate influencing the sea, which in turn influences the land: softer rocks will be eroded much more quickly than harder rocks. This in turn has an impact upon the human aspect of geography, as roads and houses disappear. A village simply disappearing into the sea is not a new phenomenon in Britain: Dunwich in Suffolk was a thriving port in the Middle Ages, yet was claimed by the sea many years ago, leaving little evidence other than the written fact that it ever actually existed. Again, ICT can assist in providing evidence of rapid erosion, perhaps through the use of digital cameras to record the ingress of the sea from year to year.

Geology

Although a separate subject in its own right, at primary level geology can be taught along with aspects of Physical Geography and Science, as well as Human Geography through activities such as the study of building materials. Indeed, we have already mentioned the importance of the rock structure in influencing various geographical features, so it is difficult to see how this can be explained without reference to the type of rock, whether it is hard or soft (perhaps introducing Moh's Scale of Hardness), and, if possible, how old it is. It is here we might introduce the standard three types of rock, sedimentary, igneous, and metamorphic, their characteristics and properties, and what minerals they contain. Some will even show fossil evidence, and of course children always find these fascinating.

It should be remembered that most of us live in towns and may not have ready access to geological sites or even the natural countryside. While we give examples later in the chapter of how we can overcome this problem in a practical way, at this stage it should be noted that in the classroom there are various aspects of ICT which can also help.

Local Geography

As with History, much of the Geography studied in primary schools centres on the immediate area surrounding the school. This could be the village, town, part of a city, or even the countryside in which the school is situated. The study could well include many or all of the aspects of Geography described above. It will almost certainly include the geographical growth of the local environment, the main occupations of the people living there and if there are any local industries, building construction, and even markets and shops. It could also involve a study of the local weather as well as traffic surveys, particularly if there are any proposed developments. With the youngest children, this might begin with a tour of their school. This topic can be developed geographically by allowing them to identify their route to school on a large-scale street map of the same area. When using an interactive whiteboard, the teacher can use the 'Annotate over windows' option to get different pupils to trace their route to school over the street map in different colours. This will teach and then reinforce the importance of a key.

The National Curriculum for England makes great play of this kind of topic, and indeed it is hard to imagine that any school with young children would not undertake such a study. However, as we have already said, the curriculum does also require a wider world view, which itself could even begin with a local study. Children taking part in this kind of study often visit the local shop or supermarket. Much of the produce will come from abroad, and none more so than the fruit on sale. Oranges, lemons, pineapples, kiwi fruits, and even grapes are hardly likely to have originated in the United Kingdom! The children can discover the countries of origin and on their return to the classroom can mark them on a world map. They can do this with many different products and in this way gradually build up a complete world picture. They can then perhaps try to discover if the trade in any similar product is reciprocal. Use of the Internet will be very useful for this, especially if authentic websites are used. By using sites from host countries, it will be easier for the teacher to dispel stereotypical perceptions concerning some countries, especially those that are deemed to be 'developing'.

The use of ICT in the teaching of geography

As we have identified both above and elsewhere in this book, identifying a starting point for any geographical study is potentially very difficult, but when the ICT component has also to be considered, then it might at first sight seem to be virtually impossible! In reality however, this is not the case, and there is much material available to provide the teacher with a relevant starting point.

When considering planning any lessons involving ICT, the National Curriculum in Action website identifies several key aspects as to how ICT can support learning in Geography, which help to provide a meaningful starting point. These are:

- enhance their skills of geographical enquiry
- extend their graphical and mapping skills, and their skills in statistical and spatial analysis
- provide a range of information to enhance geographical knowledge and provide raw material for investigation
- provide access to images of people, places and environments and how environments change

- support the understanding of geographical patterns and processes and environmental and spatial relationships
- enable them to simulate or model abstract or complex geographical systems or processes
- enable them to communicate and exchange information with other pupils and adults in their own school and in similar/contrasting regions
- contribute to pupils' awareness of the impact of ICT on the full range of human activities and the changing patterns of economic activities.

www.ncaction.org.uk/subjects/geog/ict-lrn.htm (accessed August 2006)

The site also identifies the key opportunities in meeting the requirements of the National Curriculum for Geography in England:

Key stage 1

Geographical enquiry and skills

2c: use globes, maps and plans at a range of scales (for example, following a route on a map)

- pupils could use a programmable toy to develop instructions for following a route

2d: use secondary sources of information (for example, CD-Roms, pictures, photographs, stories, information texts, videos, artefacts)

Knowledge and understanding of patterns and processes

4a: make observations about where things are located (for example, a pedestrian crossing near school gates) and about other features in the environment (for example, seasonal changes in weather)

- pupils could use a digital camera to record people, places and events observed outside the classroom

Breadth of study

6b: Pupils should be taught the knowledge, skills and understanding through the study of two localities: a locality either in the United Kingdom or overseas that has physical and/or human features that contrast with those in the locality of the school

- pupils could use CD-Roms or the internet to investigate a contrasting locality

Key stage 2

Geographical enquiry and skills

1e: communicate in ways appropriate to the task and audience (for example, by writing to a newspaper about a local issue, using e-mail to exchange information about the locality with another school)

2d: to use secondary sources of information, including aerial photographs (for example, stories, information texts, the internet, satellite images, photographs, videos)

- pupils could use a database to sort, question and present information about different countries

Knowledge and understanding of places

3d: to explain why places are like they are (for example, in terms of weather conditions, local resources, historical development)

- pupils could use the internet to access comparative weather information about different locations

3f: to describe and explain how and why places are similar to and different from other places in the same country and elsewhere in the world (for example, comparing a village with a part of a city in the same country)

- pupils could use the internet to access comparative weather information about different locations

Breadth of study

6d: how settlements differ and change, including why they differ in size and character (for example, commuter village, seaside town), and an issue arising from changes in land use (for example, the building of a new housing or a leisure complex)

- pupils could use e-mail to exchange information about features of settlements with another school.

www.ncaction.org.uk/subjects/geog/ict-ops.htm (accessed August 2006)

This is helpful material in dealing with such a wide-ranging and potentially complex subject, providing a clear pedagogy and several good ideas. In her excellent paper, 'Using ICT (Primary)', Rachel Bowles identifies several key questions that need to be considered when planning to use ICT when supporting geography:

- Is ICT being used to further geographical understanding?
- Is ICT being incorporated efficiently with the least amount of time wasted by both child and teacher?
- Are objectives about the expected outcomes from using ICT approaches with geographical data clear?

www.geography.org.uk/projects/gtip/orientationpieces/usingict1/ (accessed August 2006)

These are important questions, and they also tie in neatly with the issue of pupil entitlement. The Becta paper, 'Entitlement to ICT in Primary Geography', identifies how ICT can help pupil learning in geography through five key aspects. These are:

- the enhancement of the skills of geographical enquiry
- the enhancement of geographical knowledge
- the understanding of patterns and relationships
- the provision of images of people, places and environments
- the awareness of the impact of ICT on a changing world.

For the enhancement of geographical knowledge it says:

When undertaking geographical activities pupils will:

- ask geographical questions
- observe, record and investigate data from fieldwork and secondary sources
- create, use and interpret maps at a variety of scales
- communicate and present findings

ICT can enhance this activity by the use of:

- databases, spreadsheets, or data logging equipment, e.g. for a study of shopping, farming or the weather
- software to present information in a variety of ways, e.g. text, graphs and pictures
- the Internet and mapping software to investigate images of localities and develop map skills

When describing how ICT can help pupils' learning in geography by providing a range of information sources to enhance their geographical knowledge it says:

When undertaking geographical activities pupils will:

- draw on appropriate sources to obtain information, ideas and stimuli relating to places and geographical themes
- become familiar with and use geographical vocabulary.

ICT can enhance this activity by providing access to:

- people and first hand data using electronic mail (e-mail) and fax
- photographs, video, sound and other information, e.g. from the Internet or CD-Rom, to study another locality or environment

When discussing the issue of supporting the development of pupil understanding of pattern and relationships, it says:

When undertaking geographical activities pupils will:

- recognise patterns, and make comparisons between places and events

ICT can enhance this activity by the use of:

- databases and spreadsheets, simulations and multimedia to provide an insight into geographical relationships, e.g. river processes, changes in traffic flow or causes and effects of water pollution

- a floor turtle to develop spatial awareness

When discussing how ICT can help pupil learning by providing access to images of people, places and environments it suggests:

When undertaking geographical activities pupils will:

- develop an awareness and knowledge of the culture and character of place.

ICT can enhance this activity by providing access to:

- people and first-hand data using e-mail and fax
- TV, photographs, video, sound and other information, e.g. the Internet, on CD-Rom, to study another locality or environment

Concerning how ICT helps pupils' learning in geography by contributing to pupils' awareness of the impact of ICT on the changing world, the paper identifies the following aspects:

When undertaking geographical activities pupils will:

- use specific examples to illustrate how ICT influences communication, leisure and the world of work.

ICT can enhance this activity by creating opportunities to discuss how computers are used to:

- book a holiday
- control stock in supermarkets
- transmit information via satellite communications
- forecast the weather

http://schools.becta.org.uk/downloads/entitlement_doc/entitle_geog_prim.doc
(accessed August 2006)

Specific software for primary geography

Now that we have identified how and why ICT can support teaching and learning in Geography, it is necessary to look at specific types of hardware and software. For the sake of clarity and brevity, we will look at individual types of program and how they apply to different aspects of geography, rather than discussing how each aspect can be enhanced by particular applications, as it is quite likely that one program will be relevant to more than one area of Geography. Although many different types of program can quite legitimately support Geography, we will primarily concern ourselves with databases, spreadsheets and data-logging, as it is these that form the most powerful uses of ICT in this context. As Bowles states:

> Both geography and ICT enable individuals to manipulate (i.e. edit and visually process) images to develop an understanding of the world around them. This understanding is then exemplified through the use of data (numbers which reflect the considerable variations in weather, climate, topography, communication and culture) to highlight the similarities and differences between places and people. Unprocessed data is meaningless until displayed as graphs, diagrams and maps (all time-consuming processes when undertaken manually).
>
> www.geography.org.uk/projects/gtip/orientationpieces/usingict1/#3
> (accessed August 2006)

It is clearly (although not exclusively) databases, spreadsheets and data-loggers that can make the biggest contribution to this.

Database programs

Although this kind of program is often used to record the findings and observations from a Science topic (Williams and Easingwood, 2002), and may even be used in a History topic to record data about a group of specific people or collections of related facts, in Geography it can be of particular value to collate the many facts and figures collected from a variety of topics, such as the weather or local study as described above.

Although some authorities suggest several more kinds of database, there are three that are particularly suitable for use in the primary school.

Free text database

This is the standard search program used on the Internet, World Wide Web or on a CD-Rom. For the first two this may involve the use of a search engine such as Ask Jeeves, Yahoo! or Google. In the case of the CD-Rom the search function will be an integral part of the CD program. The search strategies are similar in all cases, so if the user wants to find out all online references to, say a certain painter, then all that needs to be done is to type in his or her name. However, it pays to be as specific as possible to avoid being presented with a multiplicity of irrelevant information. Adding a date, a first name or even an initial should help. In Chapter 5 we give more detailed advice on how to conduct a focused search using logical operators and Boolean logic.

Branching or binary database

This is a hierarchical database that allows information to be retrieved through the use of questions that need a simple yes or no answer. Its main use is for purposes of identification, and there are several such databases that children can use to identify living things such as insects or plants. There are programs available for both Key Stage 1 and 2, such as Ask Oscar which can be obtained from Data Harvest Ltd. These programs often contain both pictures and text. Ask Oscar includes a large selection of picture groups, ranging from musical instruments to sea creatures or birds. However, it also allows children and teachers to create their own picture groups. We think that this is far more valuable, as it can then form an integral part of any current class topic. The key aspect here is that it encourages the pupils to think about framing questions, which is particularly useful when seeking to develop geographical vocabulary.

Random access database

Familiar to most teachers, this database not only stores data but includes a very refined system for searching and interrogation, as well as the later production of information from this stored data. A simple database program could list the various pets owned by the children in the class, year group or even school. All conventional databases use the same basic structures and procedures. For instance, the whole topic (in this case 'Pets') forms a file and is saved in the same way as any other program application file. Each individual subject within the file is referred to as a record and can be compared with a traditional record card that would contain details of the pet listed. Each item of information on this record is contained in a 'field'. In this example this might be the name of the pet, its sex, colour or even favourite food.

Actually devising and creating the structure of a database is a very complex procedure, and would normally be the responsibility of the class teacher. However, there have been available for some time programs that were devised specifically for the primary school, such as First Workshop and Information Workshop, which form part of the Black Cat Toolbox, published by Granada Learning. These allow children, with the minimum of adult help, to collect and enter data, construct files, sort the data and eventually retrieve it in whatever format required (such as a graph, pie chart or pictogram).

A useful program that gives children an introduction to this kind of work is Numbers, Words and Pictures 2, also published by Granada Learning. Amongst other things it introduces children to examples of simple databases, and allows them to create their own graphs, pictograms and tally charts, based on any of 25 topic groups, ranging from eye and hair colour to rubbish surveys.

Spreadsheets

While a database is ideal for collecting, sorting and displaying data, spreadsheets have the added advantage that they can manipulate this data in various mathematical ways so as to produce a further set of information. For example, they can take a list of data such as the heights of the children in the class and then calculate an average, or (as we suggested in Chapter 2), it can calculate individual and total product costs, and even produce profit forecasts for a marketing project.

However, just like any other computer program, a spreadsheet can be designed for the age and ability of the user. For example the Black Cat Number Box series contains a simple spreadsheet program, which includes a wide range of pre-prepared spreadsheets for several different topics. Alternatively, children can use a simple blank spreadsheet and enter their own data, for at its most basic level a spreadsheet need only be a simple table of results or observations.

However, as we have said, it has many other uses, and children need to be introduced to them gradually. For example, the formulae required to make the best mathematical use of a spreadsheet can be quite sophisticated; and so during the initial planning stage, the teacher needs to consider their use very carefully. A simple pre-prepared program may be quite suitable for young children, with the blank sheet with its use of mathematical formulae better left until the later stages of Key Stage 2.

Although not strictly Geography but rather a linked activity, spreadsheets of this kind would be very valuable when children need to cost any of the products discovered in their local geographical studies. They are also extremely useful for recording, presenting and analysing data gathered from activities such as a traffic survey or a churchyard study, perhaps to record the types of stone or Moh's Scale of Hardness.

Data-logging

We have described this process at length both in *ICT and Primary Science* (Easingwood and Williams, 2002) and in Chapters 2 and 5. However, any project involving data of the type that can be collected, collated and displayed using data-logging equipment is necessary in many geographical topics. It adds a new dimension to projects such as weather, pollution, and even to traffic surveys. Sensors can be used that recognize temperature, light, wind direction, wind speed, atmospheric pressure, pollutants, humidity, sound, movement, weight, and pH, although this last one might be beyond the scope of the primary curriculum.

The great advantage of data-logging hardware is that it can be used at a distance from the classroom and over any length of time. It is an entirely automated process that does not require the constant interaction of the pupils other than to set, start and stop the logging process, and the computer can be used for other tasks while the loggers continue to record in the background, with no drop in performance.

By relying on the computer's ability to record data and to process information quickly and automatically, data-logging can take several forms. As mentioned earlier, this can be a quite sophisticated weather station that records temperature, rainfall, air pressure, wind speed and direction, or a more simple control box, which records more simple environmental factors such as heat, light and noise. The former requires some external hardware fitted to the roof of the school, whereas the latter needs a small box that is portable and often does not even need to be connected to a computer. This can be done at a more convenient time later and the raw data downloaded, with the computer's power harnessed to process the data into information by the use of specialist software that comes with the hardware, or a more generic application such as Microsoft Excel. This can be displayed in a variety of relevant forms such as graphs, pie charts or simple mathematical tables. Once the data has been processed into information it can then be interpreted and analysed.

An additional advantage of using ICT is that this can be done quickly and accurately. It would be extremely difficult, if not impossible, to carry out this task without the use of ICT. In the past, this might have involved taking the air temperature several times a day and then recording the information, before drawing graphs by hand for further analysis. Now this can be done automatically and instantly, so that the pupil's time is spent only on the analysis of the information, and on looking for patterns and relationships, rather than first having to laboriously draw up graphs and charts. This is important, for pupils tend not to think too carefully about the data capture, only the outcomes.

Box 4.2   Using the Easy Sense data logger to study weather conditions

One such data-logging package, produced by Data Harvest Ltd. is their Easy Sense package, which comes complete with sensors and a detailed book on how they can be used. There are a variety of sensors but the most commonly used in the primary school are those that log temperature, light and sound. The first two are invaluable for any topic involving the study of local weather conditions. The light sensor will indicate periods of sunshine or cloudy conditions, which can be directly compared to the rise and fall of the temperature readings in order to determine a positive correlation. For a geographical study, the sound sensors can be used in a traffic survey, as they can provide readings of the noise levels at various times of the day.

More complex hardware and software can allow greater flexibility, for example by allowing the logging period (the time that it logs for) and the logging interval (the time between samples) to be set. For most primary aged children it is the ability to adjust the logging period that is the most useful. This enables the logging to occur for perhaps a minute, an hour or perhaps a whole day. For example, loggers might be set up to capture data on light, temperature and sound. If left logging for an entire 24-hour period, the pupils can begin the logging, then go away and do other things, then the following day come back and analyse the information, which will have been graphed, either automatically or manually depending upon the sophistication of the hardware and software used. This means that the time will be spent on the higher order skills of analysis and interpretation, rather than on data collection. The figures below illustrate how the Easy Sense data logger from Data Harvest can be used with primary aged children.

In Figure 4.3 the peaks and troughs of the line represent the different classes' contributions to the concert. The scale up the side is sound in decibels, and the scale along the bottom is the time in minutes – in this case it is set to log for 30 minutes.

The logs in Figure 4.4 were taken at Bedford, where there was about 90% totality of the eclipse of the sun. The 'u' shaped line is of course the light, with the flatter line representing the temperature. This graph can then be analysed, with the teacher posing 'why?' questions,

Figure 4.1 Pupils use the Easy Sense data logger from Data Harvest, an easy-to-use piece of equipment that captures environmental conditions. (*Picture courtesy of Data Harvest Ltd.*)

Figure 4.2 Pupils record wind speed using a simple windmill measuring device and the Easy Sense data-logging box (*Picture courtesy of Data Harvest*).

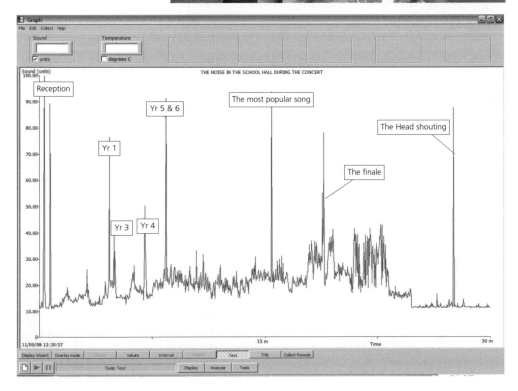

Figure 4.3 A graph illustrating levels of sound in a school hall during a concert. (*Image courtesy of Data Harvest Ltd.*)

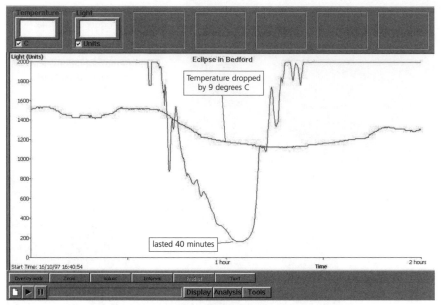

Figure 4.4 A graph to show the data logging of light and temperature during the eclipse of 11 August 1999. (*Image courtesy of Data Harvest Ltd.*)

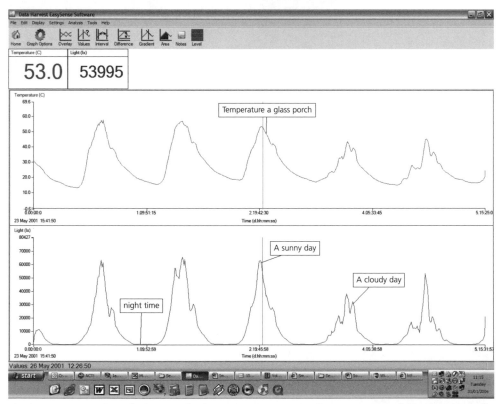

Figure 4.5 A screenshot of a log over five hours on 25 May 2001. (*Image courtesy of Data Harvest Ltd.*)

and children can explore the relationship between the drop in sunlight and the drop in temperature. This is a simple yet very effective way to compare and contrast geographical information, and ideally illustrates the advantages that using ICT to highlight patterns and relationships can bring.

In Figure 4.5 the top line indicates the temperature in a glass porch, with the bottom line representing the light level at the same time. Again, it can be seen that there is a direct correlation between the light and the temperature – the greater the amount of light, the greater the temperature in the porch. The software provides a range of aids for analysing and getting information from the raw data.

The use of data-logging hardware and software brings many advantages to Geography, particularly to any topic involving weather and the environment. It is automatic, accurate, quick, cheap and safe; it can be taken at exactly the right moment; it can be taken frequently and remotely (via phone lines, the internet); it can be transferred to another application for display and subsequent analysis; and it can provide a strong visual representation for environmental aspects that are difficult for humans to see, feel or hear. It provides a link to 'real world' contexts, and also links to other subjects: for example, the input–process–output aspect of control technology, with the sensor providing the data that acts as an input, such as a given temperature to open a window on a greenhouse.

Additionally, data-logging can aid pupils' conceptual development and improve their skills in interpreting the meaning of graphical information. As it is real information it will be firmly rooted in a meaningful context; and as the results can be displayed immediately it will enable all children, but particularly younger pupils, to understand cause and effect. In many packages a 'real-time' graph can be created, so the children can watch it being created as the data is logged, thus providing a visual representation of something that might otherwise be difficult to see. The sensors can also record very rapid changes that may normally be too quick for the children to observe and record for themselves.

In order for the teacher to get the maximum value out of using data-loggers, he or she needs to ask focused, yet open questions that extend the pupils' thinking skills. The children need to be given time to familiarize themselves with the equipment. They need to see how it works and how it is calibrated, and be able to decide when it is appropriate to use a sensor, as well as learning how to select the appropriate sensor for a given task. They need to understand that the sensor is measuring something with a value and they need to be able to make key decisions, such as how often to take the log and how long to log it for. The children need to be able to use enquiry skills of hypothesising, predicting, observing, recording and drawing meaningful conclusions.

Box 4.3   Maps and mapwork

One of the most interesting aspects of geography is mapwork, which is also arguably the one that offers the most potential for exciting work, particularly when ICT is involved. Huge amounts of information can be contained on a wide range of maps and map types. As far as the primary school is concerned, the main maps to be used and studied will be large-scale street maps, maps combining topography and contours (such as 1:25000 and 1:50000 Ordnance Survey maps) and political maps (often in the form of a globe).

The authors have also successfully used road-planners, geological maps showing the underlying rock and soil types, and even economic maps that connect with human and social geography, such as the surveying and drawing of ground-floor usage maps. These are maps where the pupils mark on a street map the ground-floor use of a particular building by using a colour key. For example, a house might be red, greengrocers might be blue, a hotel might be yellow and so forth. From this, the pupils can deduce quickly what the primary purpose of a settlement is. One might expect a tourist settlement such as a seaside resort to be largely hotels, a dormitory settlement to be mostly houses and a large town mainly composed of shops and other service industries. This can then be related to an ordnance survey map and/or an aerial photograph to determine what kind of settlement it is, and why. For example, if it mostly runs along one street it is a linear settlement, or if it is centred on a central point such as a church or green, as most English towns and villages are, it is a nuclear settlement. This might be caused by its geographical location for example in a valley or on a hill, or due to its current or previous use – perhaps as an industrial or agricultural settlement. Maps and aerial photographs in digital form can be downloaded from the Internet, and comparisons can be made with different periods of history. The children can see how a settlement has changed and evolved over the years – sometimes over centuries, sometimes over a much shorter period of time. This explicitly connects mapwork, physical, economic and human Geography with History, and of course with the local studies described earlier.

Using ICT with mapwork

Mapwork is also one of the most flexible areas of geographical study, as it can be taught right across the primary phase. Of course, mapwork is a practical activity and should always be treated as such: but as with so many other areas of the Geography curriculum, it can be greatly enhanced by the use of ICT. This can take the form of indirect support, such as the use of a Roamer or BeeBot floor turtle with younger children, by the use of a LOGO package to reinforce spatial awareness and direction, or it can take a more direct and explicit link, such as the use of online maps and mapping, aerial photographs and GIS (Geographical Information Systems) software. This is software which (among many other things) can model and simulate certain situations, such as enabling two-dimensional maps to be presented in what appears to be three dimensions. This is particularly useful with primary aged children, as it allows the 'flat' contour lines on an Ordnance Survey map to appear as a visual representation of what the landscape really looks like, complete with standard Ordnance Survey map symbols. This is yet another good example of the 'value-added' component of the use of ICT. The pupils can first look at a 'flat' map and then can instantly appreciate what the 'real' topography looks like. In the past the authors have taught this quite difficult concept through making models out of clay or plasticine, or with pieces of card, with each piece following one of the regular contours glued on top of one another to simulate a three-dimensional environment, then linking all points of the same height to simulate the flat brown contour line on the map.

Quite apart from this reinforcing the important mapping skills, it is also extremely useful for teaching the children about physical geography, especially rivers and glaciation. The distinctive 'V' and 'U' shaped profiles of the respective valleys can be clearly seen, and is an important and powerful teaching aid. If the children are going to undertake any field work in an environment such as the Lake District in the north west of England, the children will be able to 'see' what the topography is like before their visit. This will be extremely useful for preparing for the visit, and will also remind the children afterwards of what they have seen.

The use of LOGO

Before children can effectively learn about maps and mapping, they need to appreciate some key concepts. Perhaps the most important of these is the need to appreciate that a map is a scale representation of something that really exists. In the foundation stage, this will begin with a walk around the school before starting to produce their own three-dimensional models and maps.

In the authors' opinion it is essential for the children to appreciate the importance of a plan perspective, or a 'bird's eye view' of features on the ground. This means that when looking down upon a building the sides will not be visible, only the roof, which will normally appear as a rectangle. The best way of doing this is to get the children to draw round objects such as toy cars, or to make models of buildings out of boxes, draw some roads on a large sheet of paper and then draw round the bases of the buildings. The models could then be removed, leaving the outline trace. A Roamer Turtle or a BeeBot could be moved along the roads, visiting each building in turn. In our book *ICT and Primary Mathematics* (Williams and Easingwood, 2004) we discuss at great length the role that LOGO can bring to teaching and learning.

In the foundation stage, the use of a floor turtle is ideal for the conceptual development of spatial awareness and direction. It moves along the floor as the children themselves do, and they have to think carefully about the distance and direction that the turtle has to travel, and how the moves that they themselves make automatically, can be replicated in the directions given to the robot.

Another useful resource and a natural progression from the floor turtle is a screen LOGO. One of the best of these for extending children's concepts of mapwork is 2go, part of the 2simple Infant Video Toolbox suite of software for foundation stage pupils. This is a basic LOGO package that allows the user to move a car round a route by using direction and distance buttons and arrows. Intuitive and easy to navigate, the software reinforces direction and distance and the concept of a plan perspective. This is illustrated by Figure 4.6 below.

In this figure, the pupil selects the background screen from the 'new' icon in the top left hand corner of the screen. Given an appropriate 'turtle' such as a car, the pupil then drives the car around the circuit. A coloured trail can be left behind by clicking on one of the felt tip pen icons, and the direction and distance is selected by clicking on the arrows and numbers as appropriate. The teacher can intervene by asking focused yet open-ended questions, such as 'How many turtle steps have you moved there?' This will provide the opportunity to reinforce basic distance and direction skills, as well as providing cross-curricular links through number bonds.

The children can use both floor and screen turtles to develop their understanding of concepts and skills that are directly related to mapwork, such as distance, direction and spatial awareness. They can also develop other related skills such as estimation, number bonds, framing instructions, sequencing, and what Seymour Papert, the inventor of LOGO, terms 'debugging' (Papert,

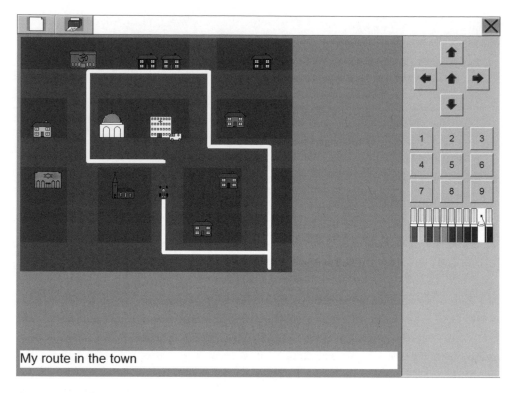

My route in the town

Figure 4.6 2go from the 2simple Infant Video Toolbox suite of software.

1993), which involves the pupils identifying their own mistakes and self-correcting their work with a minimum of involvement from the teacher. This can then be developed with older children by using angles in degrees and distance in millimetres rather than in turtle steps. This provides a basis for work that can be directly connected to mapwork such as angles and bearings, including the use of the points of the compass.

Use of the Internet

We have made frequent reference to the Internet throughout this book, and although it is true that this is a vital tool for both teachers and learners in developing primary Geography, we do not intend to dwell on it as we feel that the wider aspects of ICT can provide so many more worthwhile opportunities for the imaginative, creative and powerful development of geographical knowledge, skills and understanding. We have already mentioned how the Internet can provide meaningful opportunities for pupils to learn about different environments, economies and cultures in a way that is not stereotypical. It can also assist pupils in the study of weather and climate by providing up-to-date weather forecasts, synoptic charts and satellite imagery of weather systems at the click of a mouse. Pupils can then compare and contrast weather and climate in different parts of the world and perhaps use this as the basis of producing their own weather forecasts, which could be presented to the rest of the class using the interactive whiteboard. The Promethean Activboard has a wide range of maps and weather symbols to provide the basis for this.

Of all of the areas of Geography, it is perhaps in the context of mapwork that the Internet can play the biggest role. The Multimap website at www.multimap.co.uk allows the user to find maps from anywhere in the United Kingdom at a variety of scales, from a small-scale route-planner through to large-scale street plans. These can be used for a whole range of activities, from developing mapwork skills to studying the local environment or a distant environment. Aerial photographs can also be downloaded (for a cost) from this website, as well as from others such as www.ukaerialphotos.com. These can then be directly compared with a map of a corresponding scale, or can be used as a basis for discussion and geographical study in their own right. Pupils can identify their own school and where it is in relation to their own environment, or they can download images of famous landmarks such as the London Eye, the Palace of Westminster or Buckingham Palace.

Pupils can get a great deal of information from an aerial photograph. It is highly unlikely that many of them will have flown over their own locality at a height where it is easy to see recognizable and familiar features. Aerial photographs take two forms: plan views and oblique views. We have already discussed the plan view, but the oblique view is interesting as it shows the feature at an angle, allowing both the top and the sides to be seen. An example of an oblique view is shown in Figure 4.7.

The oblique view can be compared to a large-scale street map to identify what the key features actually are and where they are located. Images such as these are readily available on certain websites. The interpretation of maps and photographs is an important geographical skill. This particular image was taken by one of the authors from a helicopter with a Single Lens Reflex (SLR) film camera with a telephoto lens, and after developing and printing the image was digitised by scanning.

Once an image is captured or downloaded in an electronic format, it can then be used in many different ways. It can be inserted into a Word or PowerPoint document,

Figure 4.7 An oblique aerial view showing key features such as roads, a roundabout, houses, flats and a school.

or it can be displayed on an interactive whiteboard. It can be annotated by labelling using the callout options in Word and PowerPoint to highlight key features.

Another extremely useful resource available from the Internet is Google Earth. This is a resource which has to be downloaded from the Google website on a broadband connection. As the name suggests, it is a program that begins with a representation of the earth in space. By use of the mouse it can be rotated in different directions and speeds to emphasise how the earth rotates. By zooming in on parts of the earth, key features can be identified, depending upon the amount of detail with which this particular part of the earth has been mapped. For example, if the user begins to zoom in over land, key features will appear. Initially these will be fields, then other features such as rivers and roads. Further zooming will reveal individual streets, buildings and, in the case of Paris, even the Eiffel Tower can be clearly seen! Other parts of the planet have been imaged in less detail and as a result less can be seen. Nonetheless, this is an incredible free resource that should be available to all children when they use ICT. Perhaps the most impressive feature though is the search facility, where any location can be entered and the world will rotate and identify the point requested.

CD-Roms

As with the Internet, we would prefer to see children using ICT in a much more creative way. However, CD-Roms do have their uses, especially where they can simulate geographical events that would otherwise be impossible to replicate or view on the grounds of time, distance and safety. These include CD-Roms to simulate physical processes such as vulcanicity, rivers and glaciation. Although these are mostly designed to be used with children in the secondary phase, they are extremely useful for older primary aged children and in extending the more able pupils. They might contain animations of the key physical processes of these topics, such as how a volcano is formed, and video clips of a volcano actually erupting. Other pieces of software might demonstrate the phases of maturity of a river, i.e. its young, mature and old-age phases. The advantage here is that a process that would take several thousand years to complete can be covered in a matter of seconds, explaining the key features of erosion on the outside of river bends, deposition on the inside of bends and the formation of other significant features such as oxbow lakes and deltas. The profile of a river, as well as a cross-section illustrating the traditional 'V' shaped profile, can be displayed for analysis and interpretation.

Hardware

We have considered at some length the different types of software that can be used to enhance the teaching and learning of a whole range of aspects of geography. Unlike many other subjects in the curriculum, the appropriate selection of hardware can also have a significant impact upon practice. It is not always advantageous to use a desktop computer based in an ICT suite, as much of the best geographical work necessarily takes place outdoors, either in the school grounds or perhaps even away from the school altogether.

Portable devices

We have already illustrated the impact that the use of data-loggers can have on topics involving the weather, and the advantage of using a hand-held device such as an Easy Sense box from Data Harvest. This company also produces a device called a Flash Logger. This is a data-logging device which connects to a hand-held device, often known as a PDA, which is a very small computer. The advantage of using a PDA is that it runs a special version of the Microsoft Windows operating system, and also runs versions of Microsoft Office, Excel and PowerPoint. This is particularly useful as it enables the data captured from the Flash Logger to be pasted directly into Excel, so that the graphs and charts can be produced immediately.

A PDA also contains other useful features for pupils undertaking geographical fieldwork, such as a mobile phone, digital camera (still and video) and Internet access, either via wireless networks or, more usefully for remote locations, a SIM card that connects via the mobile phone network. Data can be processed immediately, or it can be recorded as an image or as a Microsoft Office file and emailed to an inbox, or later downloaded to a desktop computer back in school. This enormous flexibility provides many opportunities for the use of ICT as an integral part of fieldwork.

Laptops can also be 'used in the field'. They have the advantage of a full suite of software but the disadvantage of being heavy to carry, susceptible to bad weather (especially rain) and easily breakable. There probably won't be an Internet access available on top of a mountain either!

Interactive whiteboards

We discuss the use of interactive whiteboards elsewhere in this book, but it is worth identifying the specific contribution that these can make to Geography. They are particularly useful for teaching and displaying a whole range of geographical images to pupils. In Chapter 7 we illustrate how maps can be displayed on the screen and be labelled with different countries and their flags. This is a tremendous resource for teaching about countries of the world, and of course is best used by the pupils themselves. As a teaching aid this can be an extremely powerful resource in Geography. For example images such as maps, plans and photographs of physical features can be projected onto the board and, using the 'Annotation over windows feature', key features can be labelled and identified. Alternatively, the images can be copied and pasted into a Word document or PowerPoint slide and annotated with tools provided in these programs (such as 'Callouts').

Figure 4.8 Rock strata at Lulworth Cove in Dorset, England. By using the 'Annotate over windows' tool on an interactive whiteboard or, as in this case, the AutoShapes function of Microsoft Word, key features can be identified or labelled, such as the direction and incline of the rock layers.

Figure 4.9 A 'U' shaped valley in the Lake District of north-west England. This was formed by glaciation during the last Ice Age, with the glacier filling the 'U' cross-section of the valley. It would have followed a downward slope, probably a pre-existing river valley.

Figure 4.10 The same image with annotations to illustrate the probable position of the glacier when creating the 'U' shaped valley. The top of the glacier can be positioned here due to the presence of 'knick points', the points where the angle of the valley sides change. The profile will have been modified in the 10,000 years or so since the last glaciation by weathering. This illustrates how the teaching of glaciation can be enhanced by the use of an interactive whiteboard.

Figure 4.11 The image annotated with labels. A lateral moraine is material such as rocks which have been deposited at the side of the valley by the retreating glacier.

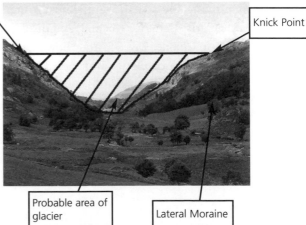

Box 4.4   A geological study of a local churchyard

This was a project undertaken by one of the authors and his Year 6 class at All Saints Church, Frindsbury in the Medway Towns, Kent. The project is detailed fully in an article included in a publication of the School Natural Science Society (*Urban Field Studies*, 1983). At this time the educational use of ICT was very much in its infancy, and indeed when the project was carried out a few years before this publication it did not exist at all, although the author did introduce computers into his school in 1981.

The case study as such therefore did not involve ICT, but we shall show how a similar project would be enhanced by its use – the author certainly would have liked to have had available some of today's technology. However, as the project was a contribution to the then National Heritage Year, it was videoed. A very cumbersome camera was used, together with a top-loading video recorder, either of which could now only exist as a museum exhibit.

Field work

In a previous weather topic, the class had observed how gardeners used frost to break up their newly dug soil into finer particles. Through experimentation they came to understand that this was caused by the expansion of water as it freezes and becomes ice. As this had led on to a general discussion about the wide scale effects of weathering in general, it was decided to start our topic by investigating these effects on the main structure of the church and the surrounding gravestones.

At the beginning we decided that there were three aspects to be investigated:

- Physical Weathering – the effects of the climate.
- Chemical Weathering – the influence of pollution.
- Biological Weathering – the effects of plant and animal activity.

Although the children could observe the weathering of various parts of the church and of the gravestones, they found it difficult to decide which of the three causes were responsible. The effects of the climate and to a large extent the animal and plant influences were often plain enough, but there was no way we could identify chemical weathering. Consequently we would note the presence of plants and animals, but measure the effects of the weathering as an integrated study.

The church is mainly built of sandstone but the oldest part, the Norman chancel, is built with flint. This is a very hard stone, commonly found associated with the much softer chalk. Flint of course is what our cavemen ancestors used to tip their arrows and spears. The children observed that there had been much erosion of the softer mortar between the flint, despite the mortar being strengthened by the inclusion of broken tiles (possibly Roman or medieval) and numerous seashells – Frindsbury overlooks the Medway Estuary. Because of this erosion the sandstone blocks and even more so the flint seemed to stand out from the wall. The children decided to investigate how far into the wall this erosion had gone.

They marked out a pair of transect lines (strings), each two metres long and reaching from the base of the wall to just under one of the windows. They measured into the eroded part from these transects (the datum line), so that they were able to make scale drawings, which resembled submarine contour profiles. As they had placed the strings at the base of the wall where it seemed the erosion was least noticeable, they discovered that the average depth of weathering was about 30 millimetres, assuming the mortar was originally flush with the main building.

Apart from showing an aspect of differential weathering between hard and soft materials, measuring the erosion meant that the children had to look very closely at the wall. This allowed them to discover other possible clues to suggest other agents of erosion, such as a spider's nest in a 40 millimetre deep tunnel. They also observed the damage to the walls caused by the roots of small plants growing in the mortar, as well as the amount of moss present in the damper parts.

Another group of children made a study of the gravestones, and observed how some had weathered more than others. On the face of it an obvious fact, for surely if some had been there a very long time, this was only to be expected? However, the children soon discovered that age was not the only factor, for there were gravestones dating back to the nineteenth century that seemed as good as new, while others only about 50 or so years old were very worn. Except for the very oldest, it was easy to check their age because of course all were clearly dated.

Research in the school library showed that the gravestones were made of about four different materials. The hardest and least weathered were made of granite, while the most worn were made from soft sandstone. Two other materials used, which showed an intermediate stage of weathering, were marble and Portland stone. Much of London is built of the latter. This range of material motivated the class to further research in the school library. They soon discovered that granite was an example of an igneous rock; sandstones and the Portland stone were examples of different sedimentary rocks; and that marble was something 'between the two', a rarer metamorphic rock, perhaps from Italy.

The lichens and algae which covered many of the gravestones aroused much interest. Why did algae grow on the damp, porous sandstone? Why did lichen cover the drier Portland stone? Why didn't anything at all grow on the granite? Back in the classroom the children carried out simple tests with small pieces of the rocks. They first weighed them dry and then, after total immersion in water over the weekend, weighed them again. They discovered that whilst the soft sandstone held a lot of water, the flint of the main building seemed to hold none at all. They observed that lichens preferred the drier stones but could not exist on the very hard granite. Various hypotheses were advanced as to why this should be so: that lichens were plants and therefore had roots that could hold in the Portland stone but had little or no chance with the granite. Obviously lichens were not too keen on a very wet environment, while after further observation in the churchyard, it could be seen that algae and mosses certainly were.

Although the children made many other observations during the course of this project, two were particularly interesting geologically. They had discovered that most of the plant life associated with the church and gravestones were species that demanded a calcium rich soil. They therefore tested each rock for lime with a very dilute acid (clear vinegar will do) to see if it 'fizzed', therefore showing the presence of lime. Most did so, although granite did not and some sandstones only a little, depending (it was presumed) on the proportion of lime present.

Back in the classroom

The other interesting 'mini-topic' was based on the hardness of the various materials, for by now it was obvious that the hardness of the material must play an important part in the process of weathering. The children devised their own scale of hardness, based on their discovery of Moh's Scale. This is a standard against which geological mineral specimens are tested. It is a scale from one to ten, with one – talc, being the softest, and ten – diamond, the hardest.

The intermediate materials are so arranged that each can mark those below it on the scale but not those above it. Hence number three, calcite, will scratch numbers one and two, but nothing above. Number nine, corundum, will scratch all the rest but cannot touch diamond. This is not surprising, as diamond is very much harder than all the rest and if the scale was shown graphically, there would be a gradual incline up to number nine then a sudden very steep rise for diamond. The very common mineral quartz is at number seven.

The children took great trouble to find materials that would fit their scale so that each would in turn mark those below it but not above. The materials ranged from chalk (the softest) to flint (the hardest). Intermediate materials included balsa wood, copper wire, and a piece of a broken knife blade. Once the children had made their scale they set about finding where the various rocks they had identified during this project fitted in.

The children recorded their findings in a variety of ways. They had all taken rough field notes or had completed a prepared simple work sheet. On their return to the classroom some wanted to rewrite their notes in a more clear and descriptive format. Others completed drawings of the transect lines complete with detailed measurements, and another group mounted and labelled many of the rock and plant specimens we had collected. The classroom scale of hardness took pride of place. As each piece of work was completed it was carefully mounted against a background of thick black card, which formed an increasingly impressive classroom display. Because of the enthusiasm of the children this work would have lasted a very long time had not half-term intervened!

Using ICT in the Box 4.4 case study

There are obviously many areas of ICT that can be applied to this case study, from simple word processing to the use of a digital camera and PowerPoint presentations. Although there are many CD-Roms available, teachers need to be well aware of the limitations of this resource. Although we have already stated these in other chapters, there is no harm in saying again that CD-Roms must be interactive and not merely a collection of facts and figures, however well camouflaged their presentation might be. Having said this, there are some programs that can play a useful role as a precursor to this and similar topics. One such is Analysing Data, which shows how geographical data can be collected, analysed and used.

Much of the information collected by the children could in any of today's primary schools be stored in a random access database program (as described above). The measurements of the actual erosion could be entered and displayed graphically, as could many of the different types of rocks they discovered, although the actual mapping of the transects might more easily be drawn out using Microsoft's own word or drawing programs. These could be drawn to scale using the transect lines as the datum lines from which the measurements into the wall are made. The complete picture could be shown in vertical or horizontal format. For identification purposes the children would use a branching database, again as described above. In this instance a valuable program would be FlexiTree 2, which allows the creation of branching databases with objects that include pictures and sounds, and is able to save any database as a series of web pages.

The Internet itself can provide valuable background information for this case study. For example, there are several entries for Moh's Scale of Hardness, which would have been very interesting to the children had it been available at the time. An address is listed at the end of the chapter (although a simple search under the heading 'Moh's Scale' should be enough).

Finally, just as the original project was recorded on video, in today's school a digital camera would be used and the complete project, including work in both the field and the classroom, portrayed in a PowerPoint presentation.

Summary

It is hoped that this chapter has illustrated the importance of Geography as an investigative, enquiry-based subject. Although facts play a part, the real emphasis should not be concerned with what is the capital of a particular country, but why it is located there: the fact that London is the capital of the United Kingdom is general knowledge, not geography – *why* it is located there is what geography should really be about, and ICT can be of great assistance in finding out. The ability to access a wide range of material instantly, perhaps finding maps from different periods in history to see how a settlement has developed over many years, is one that brings genuine interactivity and enquiry to the subject. The ability to record and present the findings of geographical investigation through the use of hardware such as laptops, PDAs, data loggers, digital cameras and remote devices, and through use of the Internet, brings a great deal to this most wide-ranging of subjects.

References

Papert, S. (1993) *Mindstorms – Children, Computers and Powerful Ideas,* second edition. Harvester Wheatsheaf Press, London.

Williams, J. (1983) *Ecclesiastical Geology.* School Natural Science Society – Urban Field Studies (publication No.51), pages 14–17. London.

Williams, J. (1997) *Design and Make – Water Projects.* Wayland, Hove.

Williams, J. and Easingwood, N. (2002) *ICT and Primary Science – A Teacher's Guide.* RoutledgeFalmer, London.

Williams, J. and Easingwood, N. (2004) *ICT and Primary Mathematics,* RoutledgeFalmer, London.

Useful websites

www.amfed.org_mohs.htm
For details and background information about Moh's scale of hardness

www.geography.org.uk/projects/gtip/orientationpieces/usingict1/
'Using ICT (Primary)', Rachel Bowles

www.google.com
Google search engine web site

www.multimap.co.uk
Multimap web site

www.ncaction.org.uk/subjects/geog/ict-lrn.htm
NCAction website

www.ncaction.org.uk/subjects/geog/ict-ops.htm
DfES National Curriculum for Geography in England HMSO, 2000

http://schools.becta.org.uk/downloads/entitlement_doc/entitle_geog_prim.doc
The Becta paper, 'Entitlement to ICT in Primary Geography'

www.ukaerialphotos.com
UK Aerial photos web site

For readers interested in finding out more about the *shaduf* and similar mechanisms, try the website of the Manchester Metropolitan University, Virtual Reality Museum.

Other useful addresses

Data Harvest Ltd, 1 Eden Court, Leighton Buzzard, Bedfordshire, LU7 4FY.

FlexiTREE2 and the CD-Rom Analysing Data can both be obtained from Technology Teaching Systems Ltd, Nunn Brook Road, Huthwaite, Nottinghamshaire, NG17 2HU.

History

Teaching history

The difficulty with this subject is to know where to begin and where to end. If we take the United Kingdom as an example, the curriculum always used to begin with Caesar's invasion in 55BC, although for many The Act of Union might be a more appropriate beginning. At the present day in many primary schools history seems to have only begun in 1939! There is also the difficulty in knowing just how parochial the history should be. Obviously it is very important to know and understand the history of your own country, but what of the rest of the world? Surely one thing we should learn from history is that we do not stand alone in blissful isolation (or never for long anyway). So it is important to learn something about the history of other countries, of the many ancient civilizations that at the time were in advance of our own in the form of their government, their social systems, their technology, science and medicine. We need to realize that many of the individuals who influenced our own history were not born here. Julius Caesar certainly was not, and neither were George Washington or Galileo, to name but two more.

How then can we find the time to teach all this? We have said nothing about social history, of how 'ordinary' people lived, how society evolved from its rural beginnings, the growth of industry in towns and cities, the integration of other cultures and religions. Obviously children cannot learn all this during their time spent in the primary school. As with all subjects, some of it will be inappropriate for primary age children, and even within the primary school age range it will be necessary to decide what is suitable for the youngest as opposed to the children in Years 5 and 6. However, by teaching the effective use of primary and secondary sources, the important historical investigative skills and techniques can be transferred across different strands and periods of history. ICT can assist greatly with this.

Planning, history and ICT

Careful planning will help to solve some of these issues. Unlike Science or Technology, History may at first glance be a subject that does not lend itself to a considerable input from ICT, for unlike these other subjects ICT has not become almost an integral part of the work. Nevertheless, as within all subjects the appropriate use of ICT will allow the teacher to make better use of the time available, will help motivate the children, and help them to assess, investigate and record historical facts and evidence. Good interactive CD-Roms will allow the children to explore any particular aspect of the subject both quickly and thoroughly, while using the Web will give them instant access to museums and similar institutions of historical significance.

While there are other uses of ICT (which we will discuss later in the chapter), by simply using the computer as a word processor time can be saved and the children motivated and encouraged to complete any essential descriptive writing. In some schools there are often periods within the timetable set aside specifically for ICT. This time may originally have been used to introduce the children to computers and various 'ready made' practice programs. Once this has been accomplished we see no reason why this computer time should not be utilized by the children for use within other subjects. Instead of such 'ready-made' programs as, for example, a database or spreadsheet with pre-written examples, why not give the children a blank database program and let them populate it with information that they have collected? We have suggested this for other subjects such as Science, but it works just as well for History. For example, children could record the results of a graveyard study, looking at the dates and names on headstones and then classifying them. A spreadsheet or database would do this quickly and would be able instantly to generate graphs and charts.

Using ICT in history projects

The Programme of Study for the National Curriculum for England for History (2000) states that pupils should be taught to:

- find things out from a variety of sources, selecting and synthesising the information to meet their needs and developing an ability to question its accuracy, bias and plausibility
- develop their ideas using ICT tools to amend and refine their work and enhance its quality and accuracy
- exchange and share information, both directly and through electronic media
- review, modify and evaluate their work, reflecting critically on its quality, as it progresses.

(DfEE, 2000)

In the same way, the Programme of Study for the National Curriculum for ICT (2000) states pupils should be taught to:

- gather information from a variety of sources
- enter and store information in a variety of forms
- retrieve information that has been stored
- select from and add to information they have retrieved for particular purposes
- talk about what information they need and how to find and use it
- prepare information for development using ICT, including selecting suitable sources, finding information, classifying it and checking it for accuracy
- develop and refine ideas by bringing together, organizing and reorganizing text, tables, images and sound as appropriate.
- work with a range of information to consider its characteristics and purposes

(Key Stage 2)

The programmes of study for both documents are sufficiently open-ended to enable teachers to plan for a range of activities while ensuring that the primary approach of historical enquiry is rightly preserved. In broad terms, this might include the use of the Internet and CD-Roms for research purposes, particularly when it comes to organizing and interpreting evidence or investigating data from a range of sources (Becta, 2003). Word processing, presentation and desktop publishing packages can be used to share and exchange information (DfEE, 2000) and to communicate and present findings (Becta 2003). Databases and spreadsheets can be used to recognize patterns and relationships, and to make comparisons between places, time and events.

CD-Roms and their limitations

Despite the wide scope for ICT opportunities detailed above, History may be one of those subjects that particularly lends itself to the use of the CD-Rom, although we should be careful before deciding which to use, and we should certainly take care not to overuse them. They should be interactive, so that the pupil is not just a passive recipient of a mass of possibly dull information. The CD-Rom should not only pose its own questions, it should also allow the pupil to answer them as well as ask some in return. It should also have video clips to actively illustrate how historical features may appear now, and have animation to demonstrate how things worked. Machines with moving parts and indeed people should actually move, and of course there must be sound. Without this the child would be far better off with a book, and indeed this might even be preferable to an over-reliance on CD-Roms of any kind.

There are many CD-Roms on the market today, and they cover nearly all aspects of the subject, from how individuals lived and worked at any given time to how whole civilizations evolved and existed, their systems of government, their social structures, and their accomplishments in such things as architecture, technology, science and art. However, it is this plethora of information that can cause problems. One CD-Rom can store as much information as a shelf of encyclopaedias, so it is essential to make certain that when children use them they know exactly what they need to discover. The CD-Rom they are using may well have detailed information about several different civilizations, all of it interesting. Certainly there are good arguments for allowing children to browse through such information – for who knows what aspect might catch their imagination? However, if they are researching a specific historical topic, such as Roman Britain, then it may well be necessary for the teacher to produce a study sheet asking the children specific questions, with the relevant guidance on how and where to find the answers. Efficient navigation of such resources is important if precious teaching and learning time is to be used effectively, so there may be opportunities here to teach search techniques which can be used for CD-Roms or the World Wide Web. This is a good example of how ICT key skills can be taught in a subject context – in this case History.

However, a good CD-Rom, or indeed the Internet, can give pupils 'wider access to information about some of the characteristic features of the period they are investigating' (Becta, 2003), and can provide 'opportunities to select and organize historical information' (*op cit*).

Timelines and computers

One very important aspect of any historical study is how to place it in time relevant to the present day. For young children yesterday is history, and even the majority of adults were not alive during the Second World War. How then can we expect children to understand events that happened several hundred years ago? It is even more difficult for them to comprehend the sequence of events that might have occurred hundreds of years apart but still a long time ago. The timeline is one well-tried method. The authors always had a permanent timeline on their classroom wall, which dated back from the present day to as far as a suitable scale allowed. In this way any event mentioned during the day, whether in a direct historical context or not, could be pinpointed in time and a suitable label added to the line.

Obviously, scale is an important factor in designing a timeline. If we go back in history for any considerable time then we need a long timeline with appropriate space for the various events, perhaps a minimum of 30 centimetres representing every ten years. This is a nice mathematical problem, which certainly crosses subject boundaries. There are computer programs which allow you to do this, but if the line is to represent a considerable number of years then it is more likely that it will be handwritten on a long roll of paper.

However, it is possible to produce short-term timelines using a computer program such as Microsoft Word (See Figure 5.1 below), or use a 'ready made' one such as Softease Timeline. These would cover perhaps only ten years or so, but are invaluable when children are making their own short-term studies, such as on their time at the school, or the important historical events in their own life span. They can design and draw their own timeline on the screen and enter the events for themselves. This would be particularly effective when using an interactive whiteboard during whole class or group discussion. This kind of 'micro timeline' project can show them how short-term history evolves and underlines the importance of scale, and allows them to use the computer in a relevant and interesting way.

The Softease timeline can be used in a similar way. The children can feed in the date scale, period of time required and title to obtain a blank timeline. They would then choose the relevant dates and write a specific caption, which will appear in a coloured box on the timeline. There is a limit to the number of words that will show in the boxes, although each box has a small arrow that children can click on to read the rest of the words of the caption.

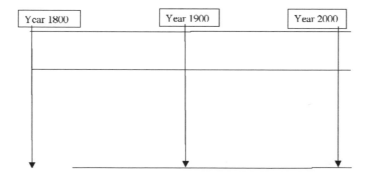

Figure 5.1 A simple timeline such as this can be constructed using Microsoft's own drawing tool. It is suitable for short periods of history or life-histories of famous people. Two hundred years is probably too much for this size of timeline, but there is some room for the most important events. The little overlap on the right hand side brings us up to the present day.

Teaching history across subject boundaries

In almost every History curriculum there is a requirement to study the lives of various outstanding individuals who have left their mark on society. Whoever is chosen for such a study, be he or she a politician, writer, soldier, sailor, explorer or scientist, some knowledge and understanding of other subjects will be necessary so that children can understand the significance of the person's contribution to world events. For example, children will learn a considerable amount of geography when they study the life and times of Columbus or Captain Cook. If it is a scientist they are studying, then they should be able to learn something of the science involved, as well as its impact on society.

This need not be a problem. Indeed, what we are suggesting is that we make a virtue out of a necessity by choosing famous people whose work will allow the teacher to design a project that will include both History and these other subjects. It will be necessary to choose carefully, particularly if the person chosen is a scientist, as we want the children to carry out experiments similar to those done at the time. The scientific concepts involved must not be too abstract, or need specialist equipment.

Box 5.1   A simulated case study

For this project we have chosen Galilei Galileo.

Galileo was born in 1564, and carried out much of his work at Pisa in northern Italy. His famous research into the nature of the universe brought him into conflict with the Church, and at one time he was even threatened with the Inquisition. This of course would be part of the historical introduction to his life as well as to the society in which he lived. Indeed, teachers could hardly fail to include something about the history of the Renaissance anyway. All this would find its place on the class's timeline.

One purely pragmatic reason for deciding upon Galileo is that much of his scientific work can be understood by primary age children, as long as they are taught in a practical way. Indeed, his work on gravity and motion is often part of the primary science curriculum, although unfortunately few teachers realize this, although they may be making a study of 'forces' at the time. This is not their fault, as the curriculum and daily lesson plans provided for them rarely (if ever) mention it.

The authors have both visited classrooms where the children are rolling model cars down a long ramp. This is usually undertaken as part of a 'forces' topic and the children may be measuring how far each car travels and recording any variation in the distance. They may time them, but this is not often part of the project, and the ramp is not the short board lined with different surfaces to test friction, but a longer one so that the cars travel quite a distance across the classroom. How many teachers realize that this kind of experiment was first carried out by Galileo, during his studies about motion and acceleration? The actual apparatus he used can be seen in the Museum of the History of Science, in Florence. He did not use model cars, but instead rolled balls down the slope. The wooden ramp is fitted with several small bells at regular intervals, which sounded as the balls hit them. Galileo measured the intervals between each. The results of this experimentation together with his work on weight and gravity enabled him to reach his conclusions about gravity and acceleration.

Data-logging

We would not expect children to be taught all the scientific details of this work, far less the mathematics involved. Nevertheless, older primary school children are able to understand much of Galileo's work on gravity: and imagine how much more relevant and interesting this work becomes when put into its correct historical and social perspective. That is not all, for children can indeed with the help of ICT get close to replicating the very work that Galileo carried out. They need to measure accurately the time taken by each car to travel down the ramp, and then alter the angle of the slope to see if there is any difference. If they first weigh each car and plot this against the times measured then they might well be able come to some interesting conclusions within their understanding of gravity and its effect on falling objects. What they need to find out is whether each car has a constant speed from start to finish: does each car travel faster and faster or do they all eventually reach a constant speed regardless of weight and size?

Measuring the time taken for the car to run down a short ramp would be difficult even using a stop watch: but by using programs such as Smart Q – Light Gates, produced by Data Harvest, even young children can make accurate measurements. The details can be read in their EasySense Q handbook. A light gate at the top of the ramp starts the timing, and one at the end stops the process. The data is collected and recorded by the computer. It would be an interesting teaching point to ask the children what method Galileo might have used for accurate timing. They will have learnt through their history that stop watches were not available to him, so what did he use – pulse rates perhaps?

This may seem a long way from a standard History lesson, but we should remember that we are learning about a famous man, his life and work and his place in the society of the time. How else can children understand his work and why it was important? Just reading about it is not good enough. To understand it properly they need, as in all good Science, to experience it at first hand. At the same time we are following the primary tradition of integrated subject teaching. This may be a broad spectrum of subjects, but as we can see here, it does not have to be a shallow one. This cross-curricular approach may not be highlighted in some published lesson plans, but as we have already mentioned, it is advocated in the National Curriculum for England statutory guidelines.

ICT and local history studies

By studying the history of their local environment, children can start their researches from the present day and move backwards in time. This allows them to place what to some extent are abstract, even imaginary facts into their own known and understood world.

We are all aware how a local study of this kind might be carried out. It could start with a visit to the local museum (if there is one), or the library, or with a talk with some of the oldest inhabitants. However, in order to discover the history of any area from its very beginnings, we need to unearth details from old or even ancient records. Some of these can be found in the local town hall, others perhaps from the archives of the local paper. However, these sources might not be readily available; they may just be too far away from the school. The Web can provide easy access to this kind of investigation.

One of the real advantages that modern technology can bring to a situation such as this is portability. By using laptops, digital cameras or PDAs (palmtop computers), ICT can be taken out of school and into the environment that is being studied. So laptops can go into the library or the records office, and digital cameras can record old buildings and other features. Modern PDAs are particularly powerful: they are small, lightweight, can run versions of Microsoft PowerPoint, Excel and Word, and often have access to the Internet and email. Because they are also mobile phones, they use a SIM card to go online, rather than needing any kind of wireless network. They often have digital cameras incorporated that can even record short video clips! Another advantage is that all of this technology in one piece of hardware is about half of the cost of a laptop.

Using the Internet to support primary history

As with the indiscriminate use of CD-Roms in whatever subject, we also feel that there should not be an over-dependence on the Internet. It is often all too easy to use it, when a little research in the local or even the school library might be more appropriate. Nevertheless, when used properly and in the right context it is an important aspect of ICT, and never more so than when used to search out records such as census details, old maps, historic pictures and old photographs. These are just some of the important records available on the Web.

In order to ensure that the Internet is used appropriately and in the right context, it is necessary to teach children how to search it efficiently and effectively. On the face of it, just tapping a few words into a search engine such as Google will almost certainly bring some sort of result. However, there could be several million results that appear to be relevant and appropriate, which of course will then present an entirely new problem! Therefore it is essential to teach pupils how to search and filter the results. History provides a good context for this, as it is one of the subjects that enable these skills to be taught in a realistic ICT as well as a historical context. In this way, pupils will appreciate that ICT can provide a 'real' solution to finding information over the Internet. The teacher must remember to point out to the pupils that these skills can be applied and transferred into a range of other contexts. Most importantly, the explicit link needs to be made between the Internet and databases, for essentially that is what the Internet is: a giant database containing hundreds of millions of pages of information. Consequently it can be searched in the same way as any other database, using Boolean Logic and Logical operators.

This 'Advanced Search' facility is available on the Google website and is accessed by clicking on the option on the home page. It enables the user to search for just about any permutation of terms, phrases, words, languages, file formats, date of posting, websites or numbers. This is achieved through the use of an include/exclude search, synonym search or an 'OR' search. The include/exclude search uses the '+' and '-' signs as part of a string. For example, typing 'National Curriculum + History' will find every reference to the National Curriculum for History, while typing 'National Curriculum-History' will return every reference to the National Curriculum that does not contain any references to History. The user must put a space before the '+' or '-' sign. Typing a phrase such as "National Curriculum History" in inverted commas will return only those pages that include exactly this phrase within the page.

When used correctly, the Internet has a great deal to offer both pupil and teacher. There are many good websites that are devoted to providing resources to support teaching and learning of primary History, including the Becta website, the 'History' section of the teacherxpress.com website and the school history website. The URLs (addresses) of these sites are detailed below. Other excellent resources include 'authentic' websites, such as those presented by the BBC and the National Archives for the United Kingdom. The latter site is particularly useful as it contains a huge amount of data and information, including census returns and national documents, often recently declassified. There are archives that can be searched online, and specialist services can be obtained via this website. The BBC website has a large amount of constantly changing information, often tied in with their television programmes.

Another valid use of the Internet is to access websites of museums and art galleries worldwide. As we mentioned in *ICT and Primary Science*, (Williams and Easingwood, 2002), this must not replace the real experience of a focused, hands-on educational visit. However, using such websites is particularly useful, especially when preparing a school visit, as it is possible to find out important information including opening times, costs, facilities for school parties and whether or not there is a shop. By looking at a virtual tour, it is possible to plan the visit carefully, as often a museum or gallery will be too large to visit all parts of it in one day. Websites such as these are also very useful for looking at museums where there may be little chance of a visit, but where viewing the exhibits will be useful for the theme or project being followed.

Further examples of ICT use

As in most subjects, it is important for young children to begin any study with a first-hand experience, or at least teachers should bring that experience into the classroom with the help of artefacts or even visiting adults who can tell of their first hand experiences. If the class is making a study of the Second World War (and most do), then obviously relevant artefacts and hopefully visiting adults should be readily available! Just as in a local history study (and this could be a part of one) there may also be a relevant website that could be used.

Primary and secondary sources of historical evidence

If it is a study of ancient history such the Romans, or an aspect of medieval history, it is unlikely that there is a directly associated web site. However, there may well be one connected to a museum, or better still an archaeological dig. As well as providing the children with information, such examples can also show how historical researchers collect and analyse evidence. The most valuable evidence in any investigation is that which is collected first-hand, and was produced at the time of the historical event or period. This may be an artefact such as an ornament or weapon, but can also be a book written at the time describing a particular event, or a diary which describes a life of a person. It could even be a building. This is what is known as primary evidence, whilst secondary evidence is what other people, often many years later, write about the event or period.

There is often some discussion about written evidence, even when produced at the time. One person's interpretation of an event can so often be influenced by factors that may alter the historical evidence. For this reason, many researchers do not accept newspaper articles even from contemporary newspapers as primary evidence. We imagine that just like today, this might depend on which newspaper we are reading!

'Specialised' historical projects

We have already suggested how social history can be taught by introducing the children to famous people from the era. Another similar approach is to choose an area of research showing the history and the development of an important factor in the evolution of society. Again we need to choose something that the children can identify with; for example, the history of transport, food or even education. One example that is particularly relevant to ICT could be the history of communication. Just as in other areas of the primary curriculum, we would wish to involve the children in drama and role play, as well as in first-hand investigation. All these are exciting and relevant aspects of primary education. They not only motivate children, but should all be an essential part of the learning process.

In a project about communication we might ask the children to imagine what the world was like without electronic communication. How did a letter get from A to B? (The teacher can choose suitable towns for this.) How long do the children think it took? Do we even need to write letters today, and if not why not?

At a later stage it would be interesting to ask the children what they think their own world would be like if there were no mobile telephones or even computers. There are some of us who can remember such a time! Incorporating all the teaching methods listed above (drama, role play etc.), the children can learn about the horse-drawn mail coach (as well as the Pony Express in America) and the advent of the penny post at the time of Queen Victoria, along with the general improvement in communication, such as the growth of railways, canals, and the new 'tarmac' roads – the best since the Romans. They would also find out about the telegraph and the now defunct Morse Code, which would lead to the famous inventors of the wireless telegraph (Marconi) and the telephone (Alexander Graham Bell). The latter would provide plenty of scope for drama, as Bell was one of the first commoners to actually touch royalty without first being asked. He was demonstrating an early model of his telephone to Queen Victoria at the time. He also employed possibly the first public relations consultant. Rather surprisingly, considering the time that all this happened, this was a woman, Kate Field. She not only kept the world's newspapers aware of the proceedings, but actually sang down the telephone to Victoria herself.

In any such topic there will eventually come a time when it is necessary to consider the most recent forms of communication: satellites, mobile telephones and the computer itself. During the whole topic there would have been plenty of opportunity to incorporate various forms of ICT, from the interactive whiteboard to a digital camera. A PowerPoint presentation would provide a suitable climax, to say nothing of a very detailed classroom timeline.

Box 5.2 A visit to Colchester Castle museum

As part of a Year 3 (age 7–8) History topic about the Romans, one of the authors took his class on an educational visit to Colchester Castle Museum. The topic itself actually began with the visit, and started with the initial question posed during a preliminary class discussion, 'How do we know that the Romans really existed?' Living in Colchester, one of England's oldest recorded Roman settlements, they quickly realized that the appropriate evidence was all around them, in the form of fragments of Roman pottery (which they often found in their gardens), key features (such as the remains of the Roman wall that once surrounded the town), and of course the many complete artefacts that are on display in the museum. The purpose of the visit was to use these primary sources to launch the half-term topic and to enable the children to understand what everyday life was like in Roman times. Appropriate ICT was ultimately used to extend and enhance the children's learning through the use of the desktop publishing package Microsoft Publisher.

Before the visit, the class of 30 children was divided into six groups of five, and each group was allocated an adult helper. Although all of the children were given the opportunity to examine all the Roman section of the museum, each group was given the task of finding out about one aspect of Roman life in detail, such as houses and homes, food, military equipment and clothing. Using worksheets (that were specific to each separate aspect) to act as a prompt and to give a sharp focus, and with the adult helper to assist them, the children had to find out as much as they could about their given aspect of Roman life and record their findings appropriately on the worksheet.

When the class returned to school, the children had to work collaboratively to produce a presentation, which was given in the first instance to the other members of the class and ultimately to the remainder of the school and their friends and families, as part of a class assembly.

At that time the museum's own guidebook was unavailable as it was being reprinted, so the opportunity was taken for the class to design their own. Using Microsoft Publisher, each group designed one page as a collaborative task. Effectively recording their findings from their worksheets, each group held an editorial meeting to decide what they were going to write. Using the newsletter wizard option to provide the page layout, the groups typed up their agreed writing and illustrated it using appropriate clip art and images. The finished pages were then collated, a front cover was designed using a graphics program and a list of contents together with an index were added before being stapled together to form a complete, illustrated booklet.

The wizard option was used in this instance because the focus of the lesson was towards first-hand historical investigation and recording, rather than simply the development of specific ICT key skills. Quite apart from the fact that producing a page 'from scratch' in Publisher is quite difficult for Year 3 children, using the wizard option meant that they could easily produce their pages without becoming bogged down by the need to spend a great deal of time getting to grips with the quite complex functions of a desktop publishing package. Moreover, the use of the wizard option taught the children the idea that text and images needed to be in separate boxes, or placeholders, and introduced them to layers. This would then provide the basis for subsequent reinforcement and development, such as ordering, grouping and linking boxes together – all important aspects of desktop publishing.

So what skills had the pupils developed during this activity? They had learned about life in Roman times using primary sources of information; developed various observation and recording skills; used empathy to imagine what life was really like; worked collaboratively; framed appropriate questions; and reflected critically on what they had seen. They then, after much discussion, organized their findings into a coherent piece of writing on the screen in a form suitable for a wider audience. In terms of ICT, they employed loading, saving, editing, printing and filing and management skills, demonstrated by enhancing their work with appropriate illustrations, borders, text size and colours, copying and pasting and importing files. These skills were developed not by teaching in an abstract, ICT-specific context, but by incorporating them into a real setting, where many other essential skills were also developed simultaneously.

The children had participated in a visit where they had genuinely learned about life in a past time by the use of primary sources in a first-hand environment. They had not engaged in the traditional activities of answering a stack of closed worksheet questions on absolutely everything that they had seen or in writing up everything that they had seen verbatim the following day in a factual, narrative manner as part of their 'news'. Many skills had been taught and developed through activities that were interesting and of quality, without the children becoming bogged down in tasks that involved drudgery, unnecessary volume and boredom.

Box 5.3   A local history project

Our thanks to Paul Edwards and Class 5 of Tewin Cowper Primary School, Hertfordshire, for this case study. Class 5 is a mixed age class consisting of 16 Year 6 and 11 Year 5 children.

It was decided that the class should find out how aspects of the local area had changed over a long period of time, and for this three main objectives were identified:

1 To investigate the local history of Tewin Village, its church and school.
2 To use Internet research for further information, maps and photographs.
3 To organize the research into a 'guidebook' using PowerPoint, to be shown to parents later in the term.

The project began with class visits to the local church. They traced its history from the arrival of the Saxons in 404AD, who called the area 'Tew's Place' after their god. The children charted its history through the Norman period, with the many architectural additions and alterations, and on up to the present.

The school itself has an interesting history. It dates as far back as 1792, although there were two previous school buildings in the village. The school celebrated its bicentenary in 1992 and at that time a historical booklet was produced to commemorate this anniversary. The children were also able to research the many handwritten school logbooks and registers, many dating back to the ninteenth century. To supplement these sources, the children were able to utilize their ICT time to use Internet research to find local maps and photographs.

The children had to plan their presentations using a storyboard. The school has a suite of 14 computers installed in December 2005. Several useful websites, and in particular the Tewin Village website, were installed on these as 'Favourites', which the children were able to access from the start of the project.

Once the project was underway, the Year 5 children, working mainly in pairs, were asked to produce at least four informative slides together with a title page, while the Year 6 children, again working in pairs, were asked to produce six slides. These children had more experience with PowerPoint, and so were able to include a contents page with hyperlinks to other pages.

All the children, whatever their ability, were able to create good quality slides of their chosen aspect of the local history. All children learned how to import text, illustrations and photographs from the school camera into their slides. Some children discovered for themselves how to overlay text onto a whole page photograph – this looks extremely effective, and examples of this are included below.

Figure 5.2 The title slide of two of the children's PowerPoint presentations about Tewin village in Hertfordshire, England.

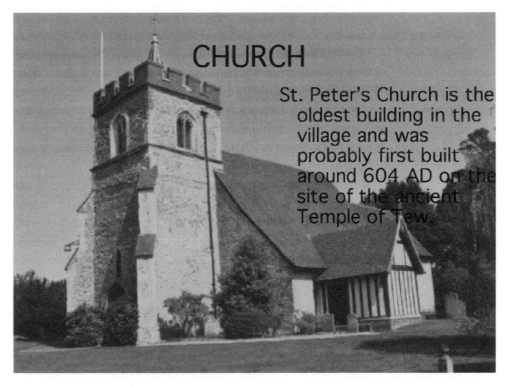

Figure 5.3 A good example of text overlaying an image captured with a digital camera. This demonstrates an effective way to mix text with images, and if sound were included also, such as music or a commentary, this would be a genuine use of multimedia supporting children's learning in history.

Author's Note

At the time of writing, this project is still ongoing, with children wanting to add music and voiceovers to their presentations. It seems to us that this is a near perfect combination of subject material (History) and ICT. The latter has been used as both an integral part of the historical research (Internet), as well as the 'pure' ICT of the PowerPoint presentation.

Summary

This chapter has demonstrated that there are genuine opportunities for ICT to enhance the teaching and learning of history in the primary school curriculum. For example, when using a database, such as those found on a CD-Rom, the Internet or even one created by the pupils themselves, the pupils can ask a range of focused questions and obtain answers that can then be examined further to learn about a given historical feature or period. These are higher-order research skills that extend each pupil's understanding of the process of learning about history, as well as providing strong cross-curricular links to literacy. These skills also involve the framing of appropriate questions and drawing meaningful conclusions from their answers, important skills in many areas of the primary curriculum.

Although this type of interactivity is not exclusively reliant upon ICT, the speed and automation of the computer provides pupils with a level of access to information about the past that might otherwise be unavailable, due to the amount of time needed to trawl through a mass of paper-based archive material. This is one great advantage of the National Archive website. Even quite young children will be able to search this site for information relevant to their study. Besides this, it also provides important background source material for the teacher when planning the lessons.

The use of relevant extra hardware such as a digital camera can provide pupils with the resources as well as the opportunity to produce an instant record of key historical features. The use of scanners allows old photographs, maps and other relevant documents to be incorporated into presentations, websites or desktop published documents. Microsoft Office, especially Word, PowerPoint and Publisher, are ideal vehicles for this. Other software, such as Information Workshop and Number Box provide children with excellent resources for the creation and interrogation of databases and spreadsheets.

The place of ICT in History is best summed up by the Becta document 'Entitlement to ICT in Primary History' (2003), which states:

> Remember the purpose of using ICT in history is to enhance learning in history. What we don't want pupils to do with ICT in history is to spend an hour typing in data, search for yet more and more information, spend hours working on fancy fonts and border designs in a desktop publisher or use every slide transition trick in PowerPoint.
>
> What we do want pupils to do with ICT in history is to see the relationship between ideas, to read for meaning, to select items, convert them into causes (or consequences) and experiment with language in presenting their conclusions and most importantly pause, think, ponder, consider and ask – why?

References

Becta ICT Advice (2003) *Entitlement to ICT in Primary History*. Accessed July 2006.

Cooper, H. (2002) *History in the Early Years*. RoutledgeFalmer, London.

DfEE (2000) *National Curriculum for England*, HMSO, London.

Wiiliams, J. and Easingwood, N. (2003) *ICT and Primary Science: A Teacher's Guide*. RoutledgeFalmer, London.

Useful websites

www.bbc.co.uk/history/
The BBC history home page. Some excellent material, usually connected to their current or past programmes.

www.nationalarchives.gov.uk/
Formerly the Public Records Office, the National Archives provides online material that is suitable for primary and secondary research, including census returns and government documents.

http://schools.becta.org.uk/index.php?section=tl&catcode=as_cu_pr_sub_06&rid=1946&wn=1
Pedagogical background from the British Educational Commmunications and Technology Agency (Becta).

http://www.schoolhistory.co.uk/primarylinks/general_sites.html
An excellent website containing resources for primary school history.

www.teacherxpress.com
This is a portal website, which provides links to hundreds of websites covering all ages and subjects of the curriculum. There are some very good links to history sites here.

www.thebritishmuseum.ac.uk/childrenscompass/index.html
The British Museum's home page for children, which includes virtual tours and details on exhibits. There is also an interactive feature enabling children to email questions to experts.

CD-Roms, programs and useful addresses

Technology Teaching Systems (TTS). Nunn Brook Road, Huthwaite, Sutton-In-Ashfield, Nottinghamshire, NG17 2HU – for many historical books, pictures, posters, kits, replicas, artefacts and software, including the Softease Timeline CD-Rom.

6 Music

Music in the primary school

While music was always meant to be a classroom activity, nevertheless in many schools it is often taught by a specialist teacher and is timetabled accordingly, even within the classroom setting. Specialist instruments such as the violin or flute inevitably have their own peripatetic teacher, and this highly specialized teaching is outside the scope of this chapter. The teacher who is prepared to regularly include music in their classroom timetable often has some skill at playing an instrument, very often the piano or, in the case of the authors, singing or clapping patterns and rhythms. Nevertheless, for many years the general primary teacher has been encouraged to include music as a standard classroom activity. After all, they teach other subjects such as Art and Science and are not necessarily artists or qualified scientists; they are not required to be novelists or poets to teach English, so why should being able to play an instrument be a requirement to teach music, at least at classroom level? Is not the knowledge of how music has evolved over time and an appreciation not only of music itself, but its social and cultural role just as important? The ability to play an instrument may make the task of teaching music more straight-forward, but for teachers who do not have this skill there is now another opportunity. With the imaginative use of ICT, such as using good software, the Internet and interactive whiteboards, there should be little reason why music can not now be a regular activity within any school classroom.

ICT and music

The National Curriculum for England identifies how ICT can enhance the teaching and learning of music. The NCAction website identifies the following ICT opportunities that are specifically mentioned in the Programmes of Study for Music:

Key Stage 1

Creating and developing musical ideas – composing skills

2b: explore, choose and organise sounds and musical ideas

- pupils could use software designed to enable exploration of sounds

Responding and reviewing – appraising skills

3b: make improvements to their own work

- pupils could use recording equipment to recall sounds and identify and make improvements

Key stage 2

Listening, and applying knowledge and understanding

4c: how music is produced in different ways (for example, through the use of different resources, including ICT) and described through relevant established and invented notations

www.ncaction.org.uk/subjects/music/ict-ops.htm (accessed July 2006)

It goes on to identify how learning in music can be enhanced by the use of ICT:

ICT helps pupils learn in music by supporting the development of musical skills, knowledge and understanding. ICT acts as a tool and a distinctive medium of musical expression, for example pupils can use ICT for recording or listening to music and for creating electronic sounds. ICT strongly influences the creative process and enables pupils to compose in a variety of different ways . . . ICT provides the means to access a wide variety of sources of information and provides the opportunity for interaction between people involved in different stages of music production.

For example ICT can help pupils:

- make and explore sounds
- record for different purposes
- structure music

- interact with different information sources
- perform and compose music
- understand musical processes.

http://www.ncaction.org.uk/subjects/music/ict-lrn.htm (accessed July 2006)

The Becta document 'Entitlement to ICT in Primary Music' identifies the following as ICT that is appropriate for music:

- computer software and CD-Roms
- electronic means of communication (e-mail and the Internet)
- equipment for making and replaying sound recordings (e.g. microphones, cassette/minidisc recorders)
- equipment that can alter sounds to give 'special effects' (e.g. add echoes)
- electronic musical instruments (e.g. keyboards) that can produce a range of alternative timbres.

It goes on to provide four contexts for implementing ICT and music entitlement (for Key Stage 2 only – there is no requirement for this at Key Stage 1, but it is likely that teachers would still want to use ICT with this phase):

- using and investigating sounds and structures
- refining and enhancing performances and compositions
- extending knowledge and awareness of styles and conventions
- giving wider access to musical experiences

It goes on to provide some examples:

Using and investigating sounds and structures

For example:

- using computer software that represents different sounds with icons that can be reordered to change the musical structure (2b)
- using a voice-changer toy or a microphone and amplifier with special effects to investigate how sounds can be changed (4c)

Refining and enhancing performances and compositions

For example:

- replaying tape/minidisk/video recordings of pupils' own work to identify improvements (3b/c)
- recording finished music work for use with poems, dance, art work and drama (3a/b)

Extending knowledge and awareness of styles and conventions

For example:

- using the Internet or a CD-Rom to find out about music for a particular occasion or purpose (4d)
- using idiomatic karaoke-type backing tracks to accompany singing in certain styles (1a)
- giving wider access to musical experiences

For example:

- using e-mail to share pupil recordings with other schools involved in a common project (2a)
- using computer soundcards/music keyboards that synthesize timbres that would not otherwise be available in class (2b)
- using special switches that can trigger sounds from limited physical movement or from expansive dance gestures (1b, 3a/b)

http://schools.becta.org.uk/downloads/entitlement_doc/entitle_music_prim.doc?PHPSESSI
D=7848a05218916115843d09327d4ceb0e (accessed July 2006)

This is an extremely useful document that also provides the teacher with many good ideas as to what can be taught at each Key Stage.

The elements of simple music-making

The majority of the musical activities should be practical, in that they involve children in actually making music of one kind or another. We have often stressed the importance of practical hands-on experiences in all subjects. Science taught from the board or book without any practical involvement is not science, will not be understood and, worse, will be a bore. Art can hardly be taught without the opportunity to paint or draw or shape materials. There are obvious aspects of practical work in Modern Foreign Languages and Mathematics, and subjects such as History and Geography have practical applications – drama, visits to historical and archaeological sites, and fieldwork. Nevertheless, there is some theory which needs to be understood to make complete sense of this practical work. If the class is making a scientific field study of woodlice, they will need to know and, because the field work is likely to have captured their imagination, they will *want* to know all about this animal. If they are out on geographical fieldwork and are shown a hanging valley, it would be a pointless exercise if they did not know what they were looking at and how it came to be there. So in Music if children can understand something of its structure, then they will be able to produce more interesting and imaginative and indeed tuneful sounds.

The musical elements

Pitch

A little more than just whether to choose a high or low note on the musical scale, this includes the different levels or grades within these variations.

Timbre

This involves the different types of sound and whether they are appropriate to the music and even if they are pleasing to the ear.

Texture

This involves the combination of different sounds not only to produce pleasing music in itself, but to create atmosphere or to mimic other natural sounds.

Dynamics

These involve the use of sound in various constructive ways to create special effects within the music. This is more than playing loud or soft music but about how the volume is graded, perhaps by starting with one single instrument and then gradually building the volume (and the excitement) by adding more instruments at appropriate times.

Tempo

This describes the speed at which the music should be played. Obviously this will depend on what kind of music it is, as well as the composer's own choice. Even within specific types of music the tempo will differ. Dances obviously vary in tempo, and a march written for a light infantry regiment who almost march at a trot will differ greatly from a funeral march.

Duration

This is measured by the variety of beats and rhythms within the music. Children can learn to use different beats and rhythms and discover how they alter the style if not the sound of the music.

There are many technical terms in music used to describe specific forms or methods of playing, which children may be introduced to at the appropriate time. If children are learning to play instruments as an extra-curricular activity then they will need to know and understand a much greater musical terminology than is required in the classroom.

These musical terms are mentioned as early as Years 1 and 2 in the QCA Scheme of Work for Music. Pupils could explore the meaning of these in a practical way, by recording sounds around the school or their own voices using the recording option that comes supplied as part of Microsoft Windows. They can play them back any number of times to analyse them – loud or quiet, fast or slow, high or low, and can sort or classify them accordingly. They can then replicate these features on musical instruments, for, as we have said before, the real experience of handling the correct equipment should never be replaced by ICT, although it is possible in the future that ICT will be the instrument. This, however, is more likely to be the case with older rather than younger pupils, although a program such as Compose or 2explore, part of the 2music Toolbox suite from 2Simple software, allows this to take place with all primary age children. At this point long and short notes can be combined with slow and fast, high and low.

For Years 3 and 4 there is no specific mention of ICT, but it talks about how 'musical elements can be used together to compose descriptive music' and 'combine sounds with movement and narrative' (QCA, 1999). In Years 5 and 6, the Scheme of Work states that music work 'develops children's ability to extend their sound vocabulary, including the use of ICT'. This involves children exploring a wide range of sources of sound to capture, change and communicate sounds. Clearly ICT has a role to play here. This might include the use of an electronic keyboard with a MIDI connection and the use of a basic sequencer, or recording their own voices, or downloading wav and MP3 files from the Internet and manipulating them before subsequently reusing them or emailing them for others to use. However, care should be taken here not to breach any copyright regulations. This may involve the purchase of sound or music files if they are being downloaded from commercial websites. However, there are many sites that offer clips of sounds or music for free. Indeed, one of the best resources for this comes from Microsoft's own website, which can be accessed from within applications such as Word or PowerPoint.

Box 6.1   Making musical instruments

Before we see what specific help ICT can offer in the classroom, we should look again at some of the 'traditional' activities associated with classroom music, and see how these can be enhanced with an appropriate use of the computer. Creating a variety of sounds that help children to understand the aspects of musical structure described above is one of them; ordering them into a sequence of sounds is another.

Before the children can do either of these activities they will need to be introduced to some of the many kinds of musical instrument. They should understand that these fall into various categories, such as wind instruments, strings, or percussion. Later they will understand that all these categories of instruments can be further subdivided: for example, brass or woodwind or strings that are plucked as opposed to the violin and bow. There are CD-Roms that give this information, but we have found that unless the CD-Rom has much more to offer, then children can just as well find this out from a book or wall chart. There are, however some very good multimedia CD-Roms that offer information about different instruments and allow the user to click on a button that plays a sound file of that particular instrument. This allows the child to hear instruments from parts of the world that would not normally be accessible to a primary school in their given country.

Although the school will be able to provide some of the instruments, most commonly recorders and glockenspiels, others they can make themselves. This is a particularly rewarding activity as not only does it allow children the chance to experiment with the sounds that they can make from the different instruments, it is also a cross-curricular activity that involves the science of sound and, in the making of the instrument, Design and Technology.

The science of sound

Energy is a very abstract concept, and not easily understood. It is easy enough to enumerate the various forms of energy, but to explain why they are forms of energy, and to describe energy itself is far more difficult. We describe energy as the ability to do work, and this can be stored in several ways. Electrical, chemical, light, and sound are all forms of energy, as is mechanical energy. This latter combines potential or 'waiting' energy and kinetic or the energy of a moving body; and they all produce another form of energy, heat. This is often produced as the result of friction, and is nearly always wasted. The challenge we face as the result of using any energy-consuming mechanism is either to reduce heat by reducing friction or to harness the heat produced for something useful, such as keeping ourselves warm.

It is not appropriate here to discuss in detail how children can be taught about these forms of energy or the work that they do. It is enough to say that given concrete, hands-on experiences of the various forms of energy, they are able to understand what it is they do, and how one form of energy can transform into another. That electrical energy is able to 'do' work is obvious when children build a circuit containing a bulb or buzzer, and even more so when it contains a motor. Mechanical energy will lift or pull objects, or turn wheels. Striking a match is one form of chemical energy, and even light can be shown to activate a light sensitive cell. They might need a little more convincing to accept that sound can do work, as it is a little difficult in the primary classroom to show the result of the vibrations that sounds can cause. However, by touching the surface of a container of water with a vibrating tuning fork, children will see how the vibrations can pass from one medium to another. It is then possible for them to understand the workings of their own ear and the part played by the vibrating ear drum. It would be a lost opportunity if some reference was not made to the science of sound at this stage, particularly if they are making sounds by beating a drum or plucking the strings of a guitar, or even the elastic bands on an instrument of their own construction. A good CD-Rom or website can help to explain these concepts in very simple terms with animations, videos and sound files.

Design and Technology

There are a variety of instruments that children can make in the classroom. Rows of bottles or jars containing various amounts of water can be used for percussion or even as wind instruments, but it is likely that in making such things as shakers, drums, or any form of stringed instrument that children will have the opportunity to experiment with and discover how a variety of materials used in different ways will result in producing different levels and qualities of sound. They can record the sounds that these instruments make, or they can make their own digital videos to explain this. They can even make their own interactive PowerPoint presentations, whereby they insert a digital image of their instrument into a slide, and record the sound that it makes so that when the slide is viewed, the instrument is heard being played.

Shakers can be made from any suitable container, and children will note that a different sound will be produced from one made of tin than one made from cardboard, irrespective of what they contain. The contents themselves will affect the sound produced, and children will soon notice that small particles such as sand, rice or lentils will produce a very different

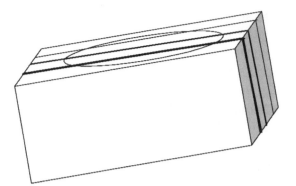

Figure 6.1 A design drawing of a simple, three-stringed musical instrument as described. It is made from a shoe box and has three rubber bands of differing thicknesses. Children will have discovered the different sounds and pitch made by these bands before choosing the appropriate combination. The drawing was made using Microsoft's own drawing program, and children can use this to label the drawing where necessary.

noise from the larger dried beans or even marbles. They can make a variety of these shakers and organize them in series according to their kind of noise – perhaps from a soft sound to a hard one, or some similar quality of their own choice. This need not reflect the contents of the shakers, but it would be interesting to see how they match. Children can describe the sounds that these shakers make in terms of the texture element described above. Although they are all made and played in the same way, the sounds produced can vary widely, from a gentle swish to a loud rattle.

Drums can be made using any size container, from a baked bean tin to a waste paper basket. These can be used either upside down like a tin drum, or better still can have thick tracing paper stretched over the open end and fixed with rubber bands or string. They can be beaten with drumsticks or finger tips, and children can again experiment to find how different materials and different sizes affect the quality of sound.

Children can make a range of simple stringed instruments from a variety of boxes with rubber bands stretched round them. They can be refined by using bands of different thicknesses, as well as improving the sound box by cutting an oval (ellipse) shape in the top or, as in Figure 6.2 fixing a thick balsa wood strip to one end of the box to make a single string guitar.

All these models are examples of design and make activities, and can form part of a Design and Technology activity. The processes correspond to those which are described in Chapter 2, in that there is obviously a need, and children should be given the opportunity, to produce their ideas and designs both on paper and on the screen. Figures 6.1 and 6.2 show examples of this.

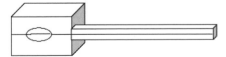

Figure 6.2 Simple plan and side view of a single string guitar, produced using Microsoft Word. Children can add matchstick frets and a simple wooded bridge if required.

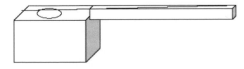

We have always stated that while ICT can be an essential element of any subject, it does not take the place of the teacher or activities such as that described above. We make no apologies for again emphasizing that children need the opportunity to experience 'hands-on' practical activities in many subjects. In this example children will not only be able to practise the skills of designing and making, they will also have the opportunity to utilize relevant ICT design programs. When testing the instruments they will be able to experiment with musical sounds, and when all the models are complete use them to produce their own musical compositions. These may only be a thematic series of sounds, perhaps to be used as the background to a play or some other form of dramatic presentation. The children can write down their own compositions by inventing a suitable musical notation of their own. This could be a series of pictures, perhaps produced using an appropriate design program on the class computer, where each picture represents one of the instruments to be played. Children will discover how they can indicate when different instruments are to be played at the same time and for how long. They may superimpose one or more drawings, and use coloured lines of different lengths to show for how long the instrument should be played. This is not unlike some of the pictorial displays of some ICT musical programs, such as 2play.

Multicultural implications

Finally, the instruments in the case study are very often similar to those used by cultures other than our own. This can give the children the opportunity to study music from other countries, and allows them to present music with a multi-cultural theme, for different cultures have their own musical sounds and themes, which can have a specific meaning for each particular group of people (Blacking, 1995). The Internet is ideal to find sites containing information on world music, perhaps even containing downloads in wav format, which can be played on most computers. Examples of Gamelan music can be searched for using the search criteria as detailed in Chapter 5 and downloaded for playing. This of course can apply to music from all round the world. Detailed below are some websites collected from the Kent Education Grid for Learning, which feature examples of world music (accessed July 2006):

www.thinkquest.org/library/site_sum.html?tname=11315&url=11315/
The World of Music

http://ancient-future.com/africa.html
Africa

http://ancient-future.com/india.html
India

http://ancient-future.com/bali.html
Bali

www.knockonwood.co.uk/

www.worldmusic.net/

From www.kented.org.uk/ngfl/subjects/music/index.htm

Using musical programs in the classroom

There can be no doubt that since good musical programs have become available, the classroom teacher, even without specialist knowledge, now has the opportunity to offer children a very wide range of activities, from simple music-making to quite complex musical composition. Indeed, their use has made the teacher's task easier, for as long as the program is both 'user friendly' and interactive, then much of the work is done for them.

This is not to say that the teacher has no input. Apart from any usual initial help the children may need with the program, the teacher will want to ensure that the children get the most out of the program. This may involve asking children to compose specific pieces of music along specific themes, making sure that they test all the available facilities and so be able to make a considered choice of such things as sound, instrument, or rhythm. Children may also need help with the presentation of their music to the rest of the class, or perhaps at a school assembly.

Two music programs are Compose published by Black Cat (Granada Learning), and 2Simple's Music Toolkit. Much of Compose is very suitable for Key Stage 1, in that it allows children to build a short melody by arranging a series of simple pictures. Each picture represents a short musical phrase, and the children can place these in any sequence they wish. By clicking on a series of icons children can choose which instrument should play the phrase or tune. They have many different instruments to choose from – some more melodious than others! Children can also alter the rhythm and volume of any tune and also pick a set of different pictures, which will in turn represent different types of music. For example, a series of typical Chinese pictures will play individual phrases associated with that country's music.

The program has a range of levels to cater for the varying experience of the children, and it also includes a number of so-called 'Jumble Projects'. These consist of a series of short phrases belonging to a well-known children's song. The phrases have to be arranged in the correct sequence so as to play the complete tune.

The 2Simple Music Toolkit program is more advanced and is suitable for both Key Stage 1 and 2. It has six programs, the first of which – 'Explore' – allows children to build a sequence of different sounds and phrases. Each separate phrase or sound is represented by a picture of the instrument, and all that children need do is to place them in a suitable order.

'Play' is a keyboard program with a choice of twelve sounds representing instruments that can be chosen by clicking on the relevant icon. The tune is recorded on the keyboard and higher or lower notes can be chosen by clicking on one of two other icons. The third program, 'Beat', is a simple drum machine with a variety of drum sounds and hand clapping. It is designed specifically to allow children to explore and experiment with different rhythms.

The 'Sequence' program allows children to build simple tunes by choosing a variety of instruments such as bells, chimes, guitar or drums, by dragging the pictures onto the relevant frames on the track. 'Synthesise' is a more powerful version of 'Play', with 50 different sounds and the ability to record them, while 'Compose' introduces children to the standard musical staff notation. It enables children to build up a melody using the correct musical notes, such as semibreves or quavers. The children can choose which of several instruments they require, and as with most of the other programs can alter the volume and tempo of the music.

Box 6.2   A class music project

Our thanks to Mrs Anne Goldsmith and her Year 6 class at St. Adrian's RC Primary School for this example of the use of ICT for a class music project.

The lesson plan illustrated below not only describes the project in detail but shows how careful planning can still have the flexibility to allow for children's individual initiative, as well as their interests and enthusiasms.

All the children, even those who were not usually musically inclined, were enthusiastic and keen to try out the program. They were soon able to take turns to play some or all of the tunes, and to complete the printed worksheet. They particularly enjoyed experimenting with the various sound effects and using them to compose their own tunes.

Mrs Goldsmith was interested to observe that some of the children, often those with learning difficulties, tended to use the keyboard to play a series of quick, staccato notes, and watched the notes appear on the screen as a series of dots all very close together. However, most of the children took a more analytical approach to their composition and not only experimented with different notes and sounds but took particular interest to find the right key for the notes that they wanted to play.

Some of the children printed out their tunes – the notes appearing in dot form – and then wrote an explanation of what they had done, giving their tune a name as well as listing their preferred sound effects. Interestingly, one child found that his tune was so long that it would not fit on the screen! At the time of writing this is being investigated – an added bonus for learning about ICT if not music!

All the children, even those with educational difficulties, enjoyed this project. They worked enthusiastically together, co-operated with their partners and remained focused on the programs, as well as any written tasks required of them. Mrs Goldsmith now intends to use other 2Simple music programs from the Toolkit with Years 4 and 5, as described in the sample planning sheet illustrated later.

Below are examples of the children's work, both from the prepared worksheet and from their own compositions.

We would also like to thank Mrs Anne Goldsmith for this second music lesson plan. Again it shows how sound and detailed planning can not only include all the interesting work that needs to be done, but also take into account individual children's needs and abilities. The lesson again uses 2Simple software, although in this case with younger children.

St. Adrian's RC Primary School	
Lesson Plan for Music / ICT	

Teacher	Mrs. Goldsmith	Class	Year 6
Dates	11 May; 18 May & 25 May	Time	9.30 – 10.00
Number of Pupils in Class	30	Number of Pupils Present	

Learning Objectives:

To explore 2Play in 2Simple Music Toolkit. To discover the sounds of the 'instruments' available. To experiment with using the mouse and the 'qwerty' keys to make notes. To identify well-known tunes from worksheet. To compose a tune and record it. To print screen of composition.

	Equipment
Introduction	
Demonstrate and explain basic principles of program:	2Simple
• how to use mouse on keys on screen or click on computer keys to make tunes.	
• how to change from one 'instrument' sound to another.	
• how to record a tune.	
Lesson 1	
Allow children time to explore and discover what the program can do. Children share findings, interesting sounds or effects they have discovered.	
Lesson 2	
Using worksheet 'Name these Tunes', children press computer keys to identify the three tunes and practise playing them. Write down the computer letters of a tune of their choosing (either one they already know or one they have made up).	Worksheet & pencils
Lesson 3	
Refine own composition and record. Play back using different 'instrument sounds' and decide on a preferred sound. Save composition onto computer and print out score.	Printer

Figure 6.3 The lesson plan

<u>2 Play</u>

<u>Name These Tunes</u>

Press the keys on the keyboard to play these tunes.
Can you name these simple tunes?

1. QQTTYYT____   RREEWWQ____
    TTRREEW____   TTRREEW____
    QQTTYYT____   RREEWWQ____

    Tune Twinkle Twinkle little star

2. WWEWT5____   WWEWYT____
    WWOUT5E____   IIUTYT_____

    Tune Happy Birthday

3. TUIO____   TUIO____
    TUIOUTUY____
    UUYT__U__O__OI__
    UIO__U__T__Y__T____

    Tune Oh when the Saints

4. Now write the letters for another tune or one you have
    composed yourselves.

    QQW QQE QQR QQT QQU QQI QQO
    QQP.

    Tune Made up !

Figure 6.4 Using the prepared worksheet.

Figure 6.5 Three examples of children's compositions from the series of options that this 2Simple program allows.

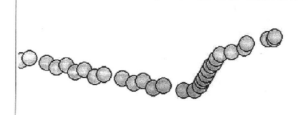

We used 2play to create a piece called up and down.
We enjoyed making this tune because it was simple.

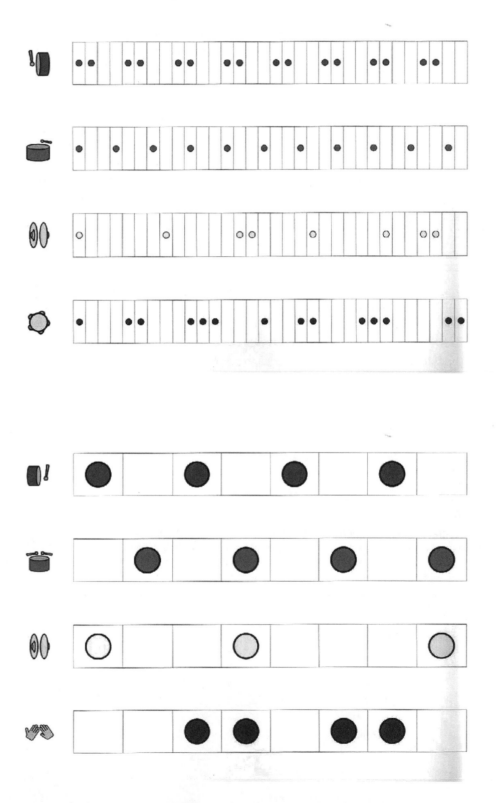

St. Adrian's RC Primary School **Lesson Plan for Music / ICT**	
Teacher Mrs. Goldsmith Dates 7June and 14 June Number of Pupils in Class 32	Class Year 4 Time 11.15 – 11.45 Number of Pupils Present

Learning Objectives:

To explore 2Beat in 2Simple Music Toolkit. To discover the sounds of the 'instruments' available and how to change them. To compose a rhythm by clicking on some of the boxes in the grid. To learn how to change the size of the grid and create a rhythmic piece. To print screen of composition.

	Equipment
Introduction Demonstrate and explain basic principles of program: • how to click on picture of instrument to make the sound. • how to change from one 'instrument' sound to another (click on corner of inst) • how to make a rhythm by clicking on squares of grid • how to play back rhythm and change tempo.	2Simple 2Beat
Lesson 1 Allow children time to explore and discover the different sounds of the instruments. Children should choose instrument for top grid, click in boxes to create a rhythm. Play this rhythm at different speeds. Add a different rhythm to the second grid. Play the 2 rhythms together. Add a third and fourth rhythm. Play all together at different speeds.	
Lesson 2 Demonstrate how to change the size of the grids. Ask the children to create regular rhythms in the first two grids and random rhythms in the third and fourth grids. Play at different speeds. Try same rhythms with different instrument sounds. Print composition.	Printer

Figure 6.6 The second lesson plan.

Figure 6.7 An example of musical staves as part of a background tile for the Promethean Activboard.

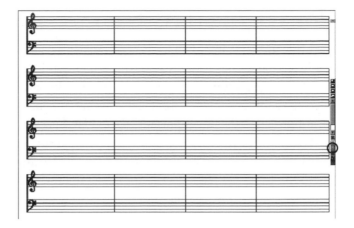

Using the interactive whiteboard

We have already discussed at great length, both in this book and elsewhere, the advantages that the use of an interactive whiteboard can bring to teaching and learning, and music is no exception. It can provide the focus of discussion for the input and the plenary, and it can be used as a 'stand-alone' tool to allow the children to work independently, perhaps to compose music using the 2Music Toolbox or play a range of CD-Roms or sound or music files. As previously mentioned, the Promethean Activboard contains a number of background screens or tiles, some of which can be used for the teaching of music. An example of these is detailed above.

Notes to go on the staves in the Promethean Activboard can be accessed from the image library by clicking on the yellow smiley face on the menu on the right hand side of the screen (circled). The 'Image library' option is selected, and then the 'Music' option from the next menu. The required notation is then dragged and dropped into the required position. If a specialist music program such as Sibelius were to be used, then the computer to which the board was connected would play the result as well!

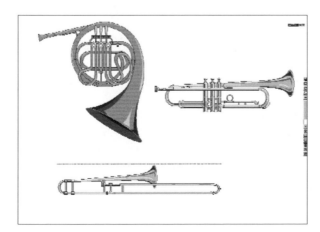

Figure 6.8 The Activboard also contains images of instruments of the orchestra, such as these from the brass section. Other images show a selection of instruments which could then be sorted into their correct classification. Which instruments are brass, woodwind, strings, or percussion?

iPods in the classroom

Teaching and learning of all aspects of music can be greatly enhanced by the use of ICT. This chapter has demonstrated that whether it is exploring the qualities of sound, making or playing musical instruments, composing music, listening to the music that others have composed, finding out about the instruments of the orchestra, or investigating world music, ICT has an important role to play. Specialist software will assist with this: much of it for the primary school is very reasonably priced and has many genuine cross-curricular links, especially with Science, Literacy, History and Design and Technology. The ability to transfer files electronically, and to download them to computers or iPods, means that music does not have to stay within the classroom or indeed be tied to any specialist area. This ability for even quite young children to produce their own CDs of music that they themselves have made is a powerful one that should not be overlooked.

References

Becta, *Entitlement to ICT in primary music,* online at http://schools.becta.org.uk/downloads/entitlement_doc/entitle_music_prim.doc?PHPSESSID=7848a 05218916115843d09327d4ceb0e (accessed July 2006).

Blacking, J. (1995) *Music, Culture and Experience.* University of Chicago Press, Chicago.

DfES (2000) *National Curriculum for England*, DfES, London. www.nc.uk.net (accessed July 2006).

National Curriculum in Action, *ICT Opportunities*. www.ncaction.org.uk/subjects/music/ict-ops.htm (accessed July 2006).

National Curriculum in Action, *ICT Learning*. www.ncaction.org.uk/subjects/music/ict-lrn.htm (accessed July 2006).

Useful websites

www.primaryresources.co.uk/ict/ict5.htm
The Primary Resources website is useful for all subjects, but this page contains many good ideas and resources for ICT and Music.

http://schools.becta.org.uk/downloads/entitlement_doc/entitle_music_prim.doc?PHPSESSID=7848a0521 8916115843d09327d4ceb0e
The Becta document quoted above concerning pupil entitlement for ICT and Music at Key Stage 2.

www.hitchams.suffolk.sch.uk/ictmusic/index.htm
The excellent Hitchams School in Bury St Edmunds in Suffolk, UK, ICT and Music resource website.

www.bgfl.org/bgfl/index.cfm?s=1&m=291&p=160,view_resource&id=63
Bournville and Coppice Green Primary School in Birmingham have an excellent website.

www.kented.org.uk/ngfl/subjects/music/index.htm
   Kent NGfL web site, also containing many excellent resources, ideas and links.

CD-Roms, programs and useful addresses

The BlackCat program Compose is published by Granada Learning Ltd., Granada Television, Quay Street, Manchester, M60 9EA.

2Simple, Music Toolkit is published by 2Simple Software, Enterprise House, 2 The Crest, Hendon, London NW4 2HN, www.2simple.com

7 Modern Foreign Languages

Learning a language

Before we consider how best to teach another language, it might be advisable to think about how we came to learn our own. By the time children start school most can speak their native language, although the extent of their vocabulary will vary. This will depend to a large extent on social influences outside the scope of this book.

Once they start school children will either start to learn to read, or if they can already do so, continue to develop this skill. As they read so will they learn to write and to spell. All teachers will be aware that these skills develop at different rates for different children. Some learn very quickly, but others much more slowly, for a variety of reasons which are seldom if ever connected to a level of intelligence – if that can ever be measured accurately. Some not only learn to read quickly, but show a natural liking for books, while others never go near them even when they are adult. Some children have little difficulty with their spelling while others find it very hard (and here we are not necessarily talking about children with special educational needs).

As children are taught the skills of reading and writing, so their vocabulary will grow. Certainly they will learn the meaning of new words as they read more or confront different specialized vocabularies (such as that of science). They will learn many new words from their activities outside the classroom or even outside the school. They learn them in the playground or perhaps round the dinner table, although the latter may have been replaced by the television screen. It appears then that we learn to speak our own language from a very early age by a process of osmosis. We learn it at different rates depending on a variety of factors, including the social environment in which we live as well as our individual rates of development, both mental and physical. Although these factors need to be considered when teaching any subject to young children, this general development of language learning is particularly relevant if a foreign language is to be taught.

The structure of language

Languages are complex systems of communication which have evolved over a considerable time. In many cases they began in the spoken form and often the more permanent written form developed from this at a later stage. Without this written form a language seldom survives.

In general a language is not a loose conglomeration of symbols, but has a structure, which in some cases can be very formal, even rigid. Some languages may be so highly structured that they are in danger of becoming atrophied, or at the very least the structure may stifle any artistic or poetic variation. English does not seem to be such a language, and we have often welcomed its 'infinite variation'. Unfortunately this can be carried to extremes, as those of us who have suffered from 'management speak' or other misuses of the language know only too well.

The basic elements of language

1   Spoken sounds, a language's phonetic system – Phonology.
2   All the individual words – Lexis. Their derivations and how the words are formed – Etymology.
3   The variations in the forms of words which are nevertheless connected in meaning, such as long/length or just a singular and a plural such as child/children and pen/pens. Or more generally how words are made – Morphology.
4   The combination of these individual words to form structures such as clauses or sentences – Syntax.
5   Word patterns and structures together with their meaning and how they should be understood – Semantics.
6   The combination of these into longer passages – Cohesion.

The elements may be common to all languages, but there still remain numerous variations that are often particular to a specific language. Such variations may include dialects, styles or words associated with particular activities such as science or the law. This need not be a form of jargon. Such activities will necessarily contain words specific to them for the sake of precision and accuracy.

Language learning in the primary school

When we think just how much is involved in learning and understanding a language, we should only wonder at the ability of average 5-year-olds to communicate with their peers so well in their own language. If they are to be taught another language then surely it would be desirable if the children could be allowed to learn it in a similar way as that of their mother tongue?

Obviously we are not going to expect children to comprehend fully the elements of the language as listed above, but the more knowledge teachers have of a subject the better prepared they will be to teach it. We know there are arguments for and against subject knowledge for its own sake (Alexander, 1988). How much knowledge is necessary? Does a good teacher always need this amount of detail? This debate is outside the scope of this book. However, we will just record that we have found that teachers who have a sound knowledge of a subject seem more confident in their teaching and are more prepared to experiment with a variety of teaching methods and approaches.

From the list of these six elements we might expect young children to have experienced at least the first four. They can hardly be expected to learn words that they have never had the opportunity to pronounce, and conversely they will of course need to know some words so as to pronounce them! Once they have a sufficient vocabulary, they could start to construct short phrases and sentences. It is interesting that the National Curriculum for England suggests (it is so far only a guideline for this subject) that primary age children should also learn to read and later write their new language. If they are to be able to accomplish this then they will also require knowledge from the final two elements. They will need to have an understanding of sentence construction and even know some simple grammar in order to be able to manipulate the words, phrases and sentences into a cohesive narrative, however short that might be. (Although for the linguist grammar can have a wider meaning, and can include both phonology and syntax, for our purposes we will define it as understanding some verbs and their tenses, so often the first major challenge in fully understanding any language.)

ICT and language learning

Although it tends to be forgotten or perhaps even ignored, there is still plenty of evidence to suggest that if a new concept is to be introduced then it should be based upon the children's own concrete experiences. As far as we are aware nobody has proved Piaget wrong. Since today's children mature more quickly so his ideas may have been refined by more recent research, but surely the basic premise remains sound: concrete experiences come before abstract ideas. If we also accept that the first step in learning a new language is to build up a vocabulary, then we should start this vocabulary in the children's own classroom, school or home.

There are many objects in the classroom that can be labelled in the chosen language. The teacher can literally stick a label on desks or tables, books, shelves, pens, pencils, rulers, the walls, the floor – everything. All these will be nouns, but to introduce some descriptions we will need adjectives. Again it may be advisable in the first instance to stay with things that can be easily seen and labelled, such as colours. A colour chart which includes all the colours in the room can be displayed, with the appropriate label for each colour. The children will at this time need to be introduced to the definite and indefinite articles (again visually as well as by sound) so that they can start to put words together albeit in a very simple way, such as 'the blue wall' or 'a brown table'. It is at this stage that some ICT support should be introduced.

Traditionally, Modern Foreign Languages have seldom been taught in the majority of English primary schools; even where they have been taught, they were often delivered on a piecemeal or extra-curricular basis. However, the DfES document *Languages for All: Languages for Life – A Strategy for England* has changed this. Published in December 2002, this document committed all primary schools to teaching at least one Modern Foreign Language to all Key Stage 2 pupils (aged 7–11) from 2009. There is no requirement for any specific language to be taught. This will of course have a significant impact upon most primary schools, where the majority of staff are not currently experienced in teaching another language. The document also recognizes the contribution that ICT can make, containing many references to it. In his paper 'Information and Communications Technology and Modern Foreign Languages in the National Curriculum: Some Personal Views', Graham Davies (2006) summarizes the potential advantages:

- Maximizing the potential of ICT in Primary Schools.
- Enabling individual learners to assess and record their own achievements through ICT.
- Raising the quality and widening the range of online teaching and learning materials.
- Expanding e-learning and providing more exposure to native speakers through online systems.
- Setting up international partnerships and using email to communicate with schoolchildren in other countries.
- Setting up virtual learning communities.

www.camsoftpartners.co.uk/ictmfl/ict-lrn.htm (accessed July 2006)

So how can ICT meaningfully contribute to the teaching and learning of Modern Foreign Languages in a way that provides a genuine 'value-added' component? According to the NCAction website (DfES), using ICT can help pupils to:

- Communicate with native speakers from other countries.
- Access a range of authentic sources of information, both spoken and written.
- Support their understanding of grammatical patterns and relationships.
- Support their comprehension of written and spoken language.
- Share work with others so they can comment on it.
- Become aware of the experiences and perspectives of people in other countries.

www.ncaction.org.uk/subjects/mfl/ict-lrn.htm (accessed July 2006)

In their excellent paper, *The Potential Role of ICT in Modern Foreign Languages 5–19* (accessed from the Futurelab website), Facer and Owen talk about the key roles that ICT has the potential to fulfil in the teaching and learning of Modern Foreign Languages. These are:

1 Increasing motivation to learn languages.
2 Enabling language learning across institutions and outside formal educational contexts.
3 Offering opportunities for meaningful practice of language in authentic contexts.
4 Offering opportunities for maximal progress in language acquisition through responsive diagnostic and feedback systems.
5 Providing innovative language engineering devices which provide just-in-time support in language use.
6 Enabling information and resource sharing between Modern Foreign Language teachers.

They go on to say:

> These aspects of ICT respond to three key issues in Modern Foreign Languages teaching: first, the need to ensure that learning a Modern Foreign Language is seen as relevant and enjoyable to learners; second, the need to offer more opportunities for learners to practise using a Modern Foreign Language; and third, the need to support language teachers, particularly at primary level, in rural areas and teachers working in less popular languages.

These are crucially important points. It is the interactive, instantaneous and dynamic environment created by ICT that allows pupils to communicate freely and easily with native speakers from other countries. For example, pupils in England can email pupils abroad, who can then respond, either in their own language, or in English. In this way, each can learn the other's languages. They will be able to see how sentences are constructed and how longer pieces of work are structured. All kinds of work can be exchanged and shared, in the same way that they can in any other subject. The asynchronous nature of email will provide the opportunity for translation if necessary and, if in contact with a distant country several time zones away, will provide time to allow a considered response.

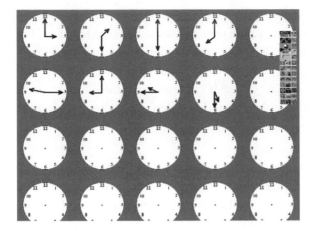

Figure 7.1 The clock faces tile on the Promethean Interactive Whiteboard.

Using the interactive whiteboard

Interactive whiteboards lend themselves particularly well to the teaching of Modern Foreign Languages. The authors described the use of these in detail elsewhere in this book, as well as in *ICT and Primary Mathematics* (Williams and Easingwood, 2004). However, it is worth repeating the relevant aspects of these remarkable tools in order to emphasize the contribution that they can make to the teaching of this subject.

The Promethean Activboard contains a great deal of functionality, with many useful features and resources. These include the 'Annotate over windows' facility, which allows the user to write electronically over the displayed screen, flipchart mode, which is effectively an electronic version of the traditional dry-wipe whiteboard, and the tiles, which provide the user with a series of pre-programmed background screens. These are very useful for a wide range of activities related to Modern Foreign Languages, such as telling the time, where the user can draw hands on clock faces provided via the tile menu. An example of this is illustrated above.

Figure 7.2 The weather map. The outline map of France can be displayed on the screen and the pupils can then add their own symbols, describing the weather in French. Again, this screen provides the focus for a great deal of discussion in the chosen language.

The teacher draws hands on the clocks using the 'Annotate over windows' option then asks the children in the chosen language the time displayed by each clock face. For example, in Italian, this would be *'Che ore sono?'* The pupils can then respond accordingly. Alternatively, the teacher could give the pupil a time in the foreign language and they could then draw the hands illustrating that particular time on the board, either by using the arrows as above, or by overwriting using a free-hand pen. The other members of the class could then discuss whether this was the right answer or not.

Other whiteboard images

There are dozens of different types of background screens that are available, most of which can be used for teaching the foreign language. These include different types of writing paper, including lined handwriting paper – ideal for demonstrating the formation of the key words in the different languages, especially those with different letter strings or those that contain features not normally used in the English language, such as accents over letters. However, we would not expect the more formal rules of grammar to be taught, or indeed any extensive amount of writing in the primary phase. At this stage, and particularly with those children in Key Stage 1, enjoyment is paramount, with discussion about such topics as shopping predominating. Mathematical resources include table and number squares, shapes that can be stretched and rotated, 'pegboards' that can have shapes drawn on them, and a wide range of squared paper. All of these are ideal for developing the vocabulary of shape and number. There are also screens for Science and Sport, and the page library option contains backgrounds for interactive games such as snakes and ladders, or provides the opportunity to label complex drawings.

However, it is the extensive image library that offers the widest range of resources for the teaching and learning of Modern Foreign Languages. There are hundreds of small images available for the teacher to utilize on the blank flipchart background, for just about every curriculum area, which of course can be immediately used to provide opportunities for teaching in other languages. These include images of animals, body parts, buildings (inside and out), flags of the world, items of clothing, the international car symbols, food and drink, places and outdoor activities (such as the beach) and transport. All of these can provide the basis for extensive discussion in the chosen language. Perhaps most useful of all are the images of money, in this case the euro. Although it is always preferable to handle real or plastic money, the use of an interactive whiteboard can provide a good basis for discussion during the starter or plenary phase of the lesson.

For example, the screenshot of euros provides the opportunity for the user to drag and drop the currency around the screen. Each coin or note can be copied and then sorted in different ways or amounts, for example to find different ways of making one euro (Figure 7.3). Other images include a map of Europe (one of the many resources with the Promethean Activboard). The pupils could draw in the boundaries of the principal countries of Europe, locate principal locations such as towns and cities, or put on the flags of the countries (flags are also available as resources, both as part of the flipchart resources and in the image library).

We have already seen that the majority of Modern Foreign Languages lessons in the primary school will be based on discussion and scenarios, possibly involving drama such as shopping, rather than based on writing, which will take place in the secondary school. Therefore, the use of an interactive whiteboard will provide an excellent focus for Modern Foreign Language teaching. However, it needs to be remembered that although it is an effective teaching tool, it is also an effective learning tool. It must be used for interactive teaching *and* learning – hence its name. The pedagogy of how it is used is extremely important here, as there is little point in using it in exactly the same way that one would use a traditional dry-wipe whiteboard.

As with all ICT it must provide a value-added component, and the interactive whiteboard provides opportunities for teachers that were previously unavailable. The dynamic, interactive environment that it creates, provides pace and focus to lessons by making instantly available top quality resources; maps, flags, money, diagrams and pictures, all of which are readily to hand and can be accessed immediately. They can be copied, cut, sorted, labelled, annotated and moved around the screen, and then saved and used for the next lesson at any time. There is no longer any need to rub work off because the board is needed for the next lesson!

The authors have seen some extremely creative and imaginative uses of these whiteboards with all primary aged children, but particularly those at Key Stage 1. But above all, as we have said before, the most effective learning occurs when the children themselves are using the board. This can either be in the form of activities during inputs or plenaries (as described above), or it might involve the children using the board independently, perhaps to read a multimedia talking story book. As with all ICT, the children must have control of the interactive whiteboard: otherwise it is not interactive.

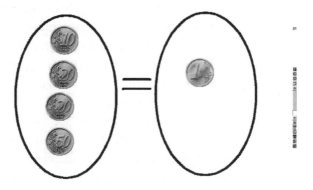

Figure 7.3 How to make one euro: One 10 cent coin plus two 20 cent coins plus one 50 cent coin equals one euro.

Choosing software

We have already written of our concerns about the use of certain basic programs that can be detrimental to other examples of ICT as well as to learning in general. We have said that when choosing a program it needs to offer something more than just information, otherwise it would be better for the student to visit the library. The program must be interactive: it must allow the user to ask questions, and the resulting information to be easily recorded in various ways. Where relevant it should include intelligent games, plans, charts and maps.

There are some programs designed just for this purpose. One such is AVP's Dix Jeux Francais. The level of language used here may be a little too advanced for many children, although it is ideal for use by the 'enthusiasts' in a voluntary after-school club. Like all good programs it incorporates sound, a necessity where language learning is concerned. A good program should have this facility, both for the voices on the screen and for recording the voice of the user. Indeed, of all the subjects that require programs to provide the facility for sound and voice-recording, teaching a Modern Foreign Language and probably Music would both be at the top of our list. Indeed, high quality multimedia resources can make a big impact with learners, providing a stimulating learning environment.

Ironically, language teaching has always been innovative in the use of audio-visual technology. Language videos have been used for many years, as has the language laboratory, a feature of many secondary school language departments. There are also many good DVDs available, which can of course be used on modern computers. By using good programs together with other forms of ICT, the teacher can now bring that technology up-to-date and into the primary classroom. Pupils can also use digital video cameras to make and then edit their own films, which in turn can then be put onto their own DVDs or CDs.

Examples of programs suitable for primary children at Key Stage 2 are those based on the Scottish levels B and E supplied by Virtual Language Systems. These start with their Essentials, which provides an introduction to any of four languages (French, German, Italian and Spanish). More ambitious is their animated cartoon program, Muzzy, which uses the character from the BBC programme. This is an interactive program that provides for recording and playback, again in the choice of four languages. The program can also be used in English, a useful option to interest the children in the character and story at the very start of the course. It includes a variety of activities and games at several different levels of progression. Besides telling the Muzzy story, this allows for voice-recording, so that children can react with the characters and even tell their own stories. There are interactive picture dictionaries, and games with a 'Ludo'-style game board for reinforcement and consolidation.

Finally there is the Launchpad series. Launchpad 2 is a disc product and was especially developed to promote Early Language Learning, particularly for the proposed Key Stage 2 (Older Primary) Modern Foreign Language Curriculum for England. This includes animated digital video programs, with voice-recording and playback. There is a choice of three levels of progression, with the emphasis on listening and speaking skills, although on this second disc there are also opportunities for both reading and writing skills. The languages available are French, German, Spanish and Italian. In Launchpad 2 the language is quite advanced but it does of course progress from Launchpad 1 so teachers can begin with this whatever the age of the children.

As all these programs are designed to enable the user to both hear and speak the language, it will be necessary for the computer to be equipped with a microphone and speakers. It is this facility that makes these programs particularly valuable for language learning.

Using other aspects of ICT for language learning

Whatever the subject, one of the benefits of class-based primary education is that it allows the teacher to use a variety of methods and approaches. This is particularly important when considering the teaching of languages; pupils learn languages in different ways, so they need to be exposed to a variety of teaching methods and approaches. With the advent of interactive whiteboards and wireless networked laptops, ICT has returned to where it should be – the pupils' working environment. As a consequence of this, it is in the forefront of delivering the language strategy and provides the basis for a multi-faceted approach. If, for example, good primary Science should involve not only observation and experimentation, but also activities such as drama and role play, then language teaching must also take this approach. We have already suggested that one of the first essentials in the understanding of any language is to accumulate as large a vocabulary as possible, and obviously this vocabulary has to be learnt in one way or another. In this way words are like facts. However, whereas we now recognize that most facts need not be committed to memory come what may, but can be recalled from a variety of sources when necessary, this can hardly be the case with a foreign language. While using a dictionary is an essential skill, we can hardly expect to carry on a conversation in a foreign language by having to look up every word! An imaginative teacher will therefore utilize every possible activity including relevant ICT, in order to motivate the children to learn, remember and understand as much of the language as possible.

Using word processing software can help here. The ability to change the language setting in Microsoft Word will enable pupils to check spelling and punctuation as they go along. As with Literacy lessons in English, teachers should employ the power of the software to cut and paste text, rather than using it for copy typing.

Box 7.1 The language of food

As we study a foreign language, so we learn more about the culture and customs of the people and the country. This is very important: taking a holistic approach reinforces the acquisition of the language by placing it firmly into a cultural context. The food of the country is one such example, and lends itself readily to the primary classroom. We have met many teachers who have organized a party for their class, perhaps at Christmas or to celebrate the end of the school year (and we have often been lucky enough to be guests at some of them). We have also known schools that have used such an occasion as part of a cross-curricular project, which not only included the preparation of at least some of the food, but the mathematics of the costs involved, as well as its main purpose, the use of a foreign language. It may not be possible to produce actual examples of the food of the country, although we know of one class that held a 'Pasta Party' for parents, who were offered two kinds of spaghetti together with Italian bread, mineral water and coffee. If this is too ambitious, then all that is needed is to provide locally bought or prepared food, but give each item the equivalent foreign language name. For example, apple pie in Italian is *torta di mele,* and a trifle not surprisingly is called a *zuppa inglese,* and so on. We should also remember the utensils. Knives, forks, spoons, plates and all the rest have their foreign language equivalents. Children will also use and learn many new ways of combining words into short sentences of the 'Please may I have a . . .' and 'Can I pass you a . . .' kind.

Using ICT in this activity

This can begin before the party starts. Children can design a colourful menu, using a good art program such as Granada Learning's (Black Cat) Fresco.

Writing with a mouse is quite difficult, even for adults, but there is nothing to stop children from using design programs that allow for standard printing, or even using Microsoft's own Draw program. This written menu could have used different fonts or it could be written in italics. The menu example shown below was of course originally in a mixture of colours (in this instance mainly reds, blues and green). Although it is likely that French will be the foreign language being taught, we have chosen Italian as one of the other options provided on most language programs.

During the preparation for the meal, the children can also calculate the cost of the materials used. It might be that this is a party open to friends and parents, with the intention of raising money for charity or even school funds. They will therefore need to calculate not only the costs involved but also what charges should be made to cover the costs and to make a fair and reasonable profit. This can be done by using a spreadsheet program such as in Information Toolbox. While the numbers may stay the same and costs be calculated in sterling (although there is no reason why final costs at least should not be converted into euros), the names of each item should be entered where required in the relevant foreign language. Hence ten containers of 500 grams of ice cream will be entered as *dieci contenitori di cinquecento grammi di gelato,* and then calculated using the spreadsheet's own formula.

Although at the start of this chapter we have suggested that Modern Foreign Language teaching, particularly with young children, is essentially a spoken subject, we have found that there comes a time when children not only need but want to write down at least some of this new language. It is, as we have said, part of the evolutionary process of learning. We trust that these activities give such an opportunity in both a constructive and enjoyable way.

Finally, as with any special event a record can be made using the school's digital camera, or a complete digital presentation can even be produced using a PowerPoint program, with of course any screen writing in the relevant foreign language.

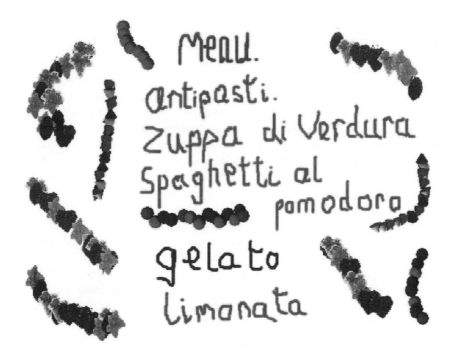

Figure 7.4 A simple menu using the design program Fresco.

Box 7.2   Shopping in a foreign language

Shopping is a standard part of most Key Stage 1 children's education: and a classroom shop, together with artificial produce and plastic money, is still a common sight in many primary schools. A classroom shop of this kind may be irrelevant for older children, who do their own shopping at the supermarket anyway. However, if it was used to help teach a foreign language then it could be a valuable resource. This is not a new idea, although ironically our first encounter with it involved its use in an Italian school, where the children were of course learning English (Spila, 1990).

It would be ideal if the goods could be priced in euros, the most likely currency used by any of the countries whose languages the children will be studying. In this way the children will be introduced to money and numbers in the foreign language (as suggested earlier in this chapter). All the goods can be labelled as well as priced, and suitable programs such as Fresco can be used to design and print all the notices, prices, special offers, advertisements, perhaps even a 'Recipe of the Day'.

A continual record of costs can be made, and by using a spreadsheet such as we describe below, a complete audit can be produced each term (or whenever the teacher decides is a suitable time), which would not only show costs and profit margins, but could be used by older children to calculate such things as 'best buys' and even decide if any product should be discontinued as 'not profitable'. All this would be a very relevant reinforcement for their language learning as well as enhancing their computer and mathematical skills.

> ## Box 7.3 Using spreadsheets and database programs
>
> We have described these in some detail in a previous book (*ICT and Primary Science*), although by now most teachers will be well practised in their use. We have already suggested that the costing of a party or a shop should be carried out using a spreadsheet, with information added in the appropriate foreign language. If children can manage this activity, then there is no reason why they should not attempt to produce a database in the same language.
>
> For suitable database programs we have previously suggested using Black Cat (Granada Learning) Toolbox. Toolbox contains both First Workshop and Information Workshop, the former suitable for younger children, while the latter is more appropriate for Key Stage 2, and allows for differentiation by providing three differing levels of sophistication.
>
> Although these programs have their own 'ready-made' databases, we have always advocated that once the children have used these to acquaint themselves with the procedures necessary to build a database, they should make their own, from their own data that they have collected themselves. They may already have built a database program that shows the various pets owned by the members of the class, or better still the year group or indeed the whole school (as the more information a database holds the more relevant it becomes). The children could construct this database but instead of using English names for cat, dog, rabbit or the other pets, these names should be replaced with the foreign language equivalent. Field names for the database would also be in this language, so that the vocabulary would eventually include colours, types of food, age, or even size and weight. As long as the vocabulary is at an appropriate level for the children there is no reason why other similar projects should not be attempted. A transport survey in a foreign language would be a very interesting challenge.

Language, drama and ICT

We have often advocated the use of drama in a variety of subjects, such as History and even Science. Drama and role play help the children to appreciate the social conditions of any particular historical period, and how these may have affected the particular characters they play. In both History and Science, drama can be a way of making real to children the lives of famous people, and in Science it can help children to understand, in an enjoyable and constructive way, many difficult abstract concepts.

Drama has already been used in the teaching of different languages. The Cambridge Classics Project incorporated it into their Latin teaching several years ago. The Project is a course designed to interest and motivate children in a language normally associated with a didactic, rote learning style of teaching. Latin is not a modern language: but the principle of using drama as one of the aspects of teaching and learning remains the same.

We are not suggesting a long play, but it is possible for children to write a script for a short presentation (just as they might for any class assembly) about a foreign country that is written in the language of that country. For example, it could show aspects of primary education in that country and explain how these might differ from our own. The children (or at least some of them) could write the script using computers and produce print-outs for the other members of the cast. They might even produce an English translation for the audience, although this could be shown on an interactive whiteboard if one was available. As with all these kinds of events the school's digital camera can be used, and a PowerPoint presentation is always an option.

Foreign languages and the Internet

Searching the Internet, like viewing too many information-only CD-Roms, can be a time-consuming and unproductive exercise. However, if the teacher or indeed the pupil has a specific requirement in mind so that they can focus on a particular site or even one aspect of a site, then this can provide useful information. Economic details, population and birth rates, various aspects of a country's geography, education system and political and social culture can all provide a background for the learning of the language and an understanding of the people who speak it. Museum and gallery websites can also provide an insight into the artistic and scientific achievements of the country concerned. Although the teacher needs to consider the validity of websites for Modern Foreign Languages in the same way that they would for other subjects, the use of authentic websites can provide effective resources, providing 'real' information in the language concerned. This effectiveness will be significantly enhanced by using search criteria (as described in Chapter 5).

Finally, if it is possible to communicate with a similar school in another country, then there will be a practical and necessary reason to learn more of the language. Pupils would be obliged to send their messages in the language spoken in the receiving school. This is a difficult but very enjoyable activity, and one that has considerable potential for learning. A text-messaging program such as Microsoft Messenger would be ideal for this.

Summary

It is hoped that this chapter will have illustrated that there is a great deal of potential for enhancing the teaching and learning of Modern Foreign Languages with ICT. As we have already discussed elsewhere in this book, it is important that ICT is used in the correct way. Although there is a danger of this not happening with all subjects, there is possibly greater scope for it to be used incorrectly with Modern Foreign Languages. Certainly we have already commented on the use of the language laboratory as an early example of educational teaching, as well as giving some examples of suitable CD-Roms. However, the potential exists for the pupils to become passive recipients of the target language, wearing headphones and working in isolation with little or no interaction other than repeating words or phrases back to the computer.

Hopefully this chapter will have illustrated that this need not be the case, and that even 'old style' technology can be used in an imaginative and creative way. The use of modern multimedia software, and in particular the ability to integrate information from a number of sources, provides genuine opportunities for interactive teaching and learning. By using the many functions of the computer, particularly the ability to record and playback sound, download images and video that can then subsequently be edited, and to run multimedia software, language teaching can be delivered in an exciting and dynamic way. Above all, it is important to place whatever language is being taught firmly in the context of the culture that it represents, as this will ensure an effective use of ICT through the need to learn about other countries and the people that live in them.

References

Alexander, R. (1988) *Primary Teaching* (Second Edition). Cassell, London.

Davies, G. 'Information and Communications Technology and Modern Foreign Languages in the National Curriculum: Some Personal Views' (accessed July 2006) www.camsoftpartners.co.uk/ictmfl/ict-lrn.htm

DfES (1999) *The National Curriculum for England, Handbook for Primary Teachers, Key Stages 1 and 2.*

Spila, A. (1990) 'A Language Workshop', *Jet Magazine*. Vol.1 No.1, page 17.

Williams, J., and Easingwood, N. (2003) *ICT and Primary Mathematics,* RoutledgeFalmer, London.

Useful websites

www.cambridgeSCP.com
 Cambridge Classics Project website

www.cilt.org.uk
 National Centre for Languages website

www.dfes.gov.uk/languagesstrategy/pdf/DfESLanguagesStrategy.pdf
 DfES language strategy

www.ict4lt.org/
 The ICT for Language Training website, which contains a collection of free training materials and resources.

www.itscotland.org.uk
 5–14 National Language Guidelines (Scotland)

www.languages-ict.org.uk
 A website dedicated to using ICT with Modern Foreign Languages, which includes ideas and resources.

www.nacell.org.uk/index.htm
  The National Advisory Centre for Early Language Learning website

www.ncaction.org.uk/subjects/mfl/ict-lrn.htm
  The National Curriculum in Action website

www.vls-onlineschool.com
  Language products from VL systems.

CD-Roms, programs and useful addresses

The CD-Roms Essentials, Muzzy, and Launchpad can be obtained from Virtual Language Systems Ltd, Park House, 5 Park Road, Chorley, Lancashire, PR7 1QU.

The program Dix Jeux Francais is published by AVP, School Hill Centre, Chepstow, Monmouthshire, NP16 5PH. There are other similar and equally useful games programs in this series for Spanish and German. www.avp.co.uk

The programs Fresco, used for the first of the menus above, and Toolbox are published by Black Cat, Granada Learning Ltd, Granada Television, Quay Street, Manchester, M60 9EA.

Schools interested in working with similar schools abroad should first contact for advice an organization such as The Association for Language Learning, 150 Railway Terrace, Rugby, CV21 2HN, UK. www.all-language.org.uk

8 Physical Education

Physical education in the primary curriculum

Along with the other Foundation Subjects, PE has tended in recent years to be 'squeezed' out of the curriculum by a focus on the core subjects. This has been further compounded by the fact that some schools have sold off their playing fields for building land (a considerable source of income in these times of financial shortage), and by a lack of confidence in teaching the different aspects of PE from some teachers, together with the threat of legal action if a child gets injured.

This is a great pity, as primary aged children are naturally active and PE provides the opportunity for them to harness their energy in a way that is both constructive and creative. Considering the issue of obesity in some children it must be appreciated that the role of PE in the primary curriculum has seldom been more important. The aspect of health-related fitness is an extremely important one, as children have plenty of energy to expend – any teacher will tell you what their classrooms are like when the children miss outside play because of bad weather! PE provides pupils with the opportunity to expend their energy while learning about their bodies in a manner that is organized and structured.

In the primary school, PE is usually composed of the following four elements:

- Dance – usually in the form of movement.
- Gymnastics – involving the floor, small apparatus and large apparatus.

- Games – focusing on key skills such as kicking, throwing, striking and catching which can then subsequently be incorporated into specific sports such as football, cricket, rounders and tennis.
- Swimming.

We will not discuss the place of swimming in this chapter. This is for two good reasons; first, it is often taught by a specialist swimming teacher and second, there are few opportunities for ICT to be incorporated anyway. Consequently we will focus upon the other three areas, as there are plenty of opportunities to use ICT to enhance teaching and learning in Dance, Gymnastics and Games.

ICT and Physical Education

Given the practical and/or outdoors nature of the subject, it might appear at first glance that ICT can make little significant contribution to PE. Indeed, it might seem that of all the Foundation Subjects this is the one that arguably relies on ICT the least. Even the National Curriculum for England recognizes this, by making minimal reference to it, with three of the four suggested examples of the use of ICT involving the use of video recordings. While we have no objection to these being used, we feel that ICT should primarily involve work with computers and their peripherals, with the pupils taking the lead in their use. Given that the use of relevant hardware and software can play such an imaginative and interesting role in all subjects and especially PE, we are going to concentrate on these, and take the video recordings for granted.

There is, for example, other hardware such as interactive whiteboards and digital video cameras available, as well as cheap and easy-to-use editing software which provides a significant opportunity for ICT to be used in several interesting and imaginative ways with PE. The National Curriculum in Action website for PE states that ICT can assist learning as:

> ICT helps pupils learn in PE by promoting and developing ownership of their work and the directions they choose to take. This can have a positive effect on their motivation and degree of engagement in their work. It helps in their choice of learning style and so promotes greater independence.

It goes on to say that ICT can develop and enhance the children's abilities to:

- think in different ways so that they can select and apply skills, tactics and compositional ideas, and evaluate and improve performance
- collect, analyse and interpret data
- take on a wider range of roles and responsibilities in PE, sport and dance settings
- access a range of information sources to enhance knowledge in PE and its connections and applications in other areas of learning

- access a range of information sources to enhance knowledge in PE such as anatomy, physiology, sport in society, health and well-being, and skills and techniques specific to activities
- support their understanding of the importance of PE and the importance of health, sport, and the performing arts in the culture of our society and the global community
- access images of performance enhancing knowledge of skill, strategy, choreography/composition, and physical training and conditioning
- increase their awareness of the impact of ICT on the changing world.

www.ncaction.org.uk/subjects/pe/ict-lrn.htm (accessed August 2006)

The National Curriculum in Action website goes on to identify the following opportunities that ICT can bring to the PE programme of study:

Key stage 1

6 Dance activities

- Pupils could use videos of movements and actions to develop their ideas.

8 Gymnastic activities

- Pupils could use videos of movements and actions to develop their ideas.
- Pupils could use a concept keyboard to record the order of specific actions in their sequences.

Key stage 2

6 Dance activities

- Pupils could use video recordings of their sequences and dances to compare ideas and quality.
- Pupils could use video and CD-Roms of actions, balances and body shapes to improve performance.

8 Gymnastic activities

- Pupils could use video recordings of their sequences and dances to compare ideas and quality.
- Pupils could use video and CD-Roms of actions, balances and body shapes to improve performance.

10 Athletic activities

- Pupils could use video and CD-Roms of actions, balances and body shapes to improve performance.

http://www.ncaction.org.uk/subjects/pe/ict-ops.htm (accessed August 2006)

In the view of the authors, these represent rather limited ideas and opportunities. Interestingly, the use of spreadsheets is not mentioned until Key Stages 3 and 4. This is perhaps a little surprising, as there are several meaningful opportunities to develop health-related fitness work. For example, pupils can exercise for one minute and then count their pulse rates, which can be recorded on a spreadsheet. This could be repeated several times and then graphed and compared with other members of the class. This will be described in more detail later.

Detailed below are the principal uses that we think ICT can fulfil in supporting PE.

Digital video

This represents one of the most exciting recent developments in ICT hardware. Although digital video brings an enormous amount of 'value-added' ICT to all subjects, PE probably benefits more than most. This is because other subjects (such as History or Geography) tend to use digital video as a tool, to record pupil work or static features such as buildings or scenery. However, in PE this is taken one stage further by using it as a means of analysing the outcomes of pupil work with a view to improving future performance. This is particularly important with a subject such as PE, as any kind of movement that the child creates in dance, gymnastics or games will be lost as soon as it is finished and will be difficult or impossible to replicate. With 30 or more children all performing actions at once in a lesson, both children and the teacher miss the vast majority of work produced.

The use of a digital video camera goes some way to eliminate this, as the children can capture their actions and immediately view what has been recorded by playing back what they have done on the camera's built-in screen. If they do not want to keep it they can record over it straight away, or alternatively, they can keep it and download it to a computer later on for editing. Digital video-editing software can then be used to create their own films by editing their 'raw' footage. These can be enhanced with the use of titles, sound, music, and transitions between scenes, and can also have a wide range of visual effects added. Very professional-looking films can be created in a very short space of time – indeed, what would have taken several professional film editors several days to produce can now be achieved in a couple of hours! This is extremely powerful, and can make a significant impact on teaching and learning in all aspects of PE.

There follows a step-by-step guide showing how to use digital video.

Step 1   Learning how to use the camera

Digital video cameras are extremely easy to use, and even children in Key Stage 1 can use them with a minimum of instruction. A relatively inexpensive device, the camera is usually small and light, so a child can hold it in one hand, with footage being captured by pressing down a button on the top of the camera. There is also usually a rocker switch on the front of the camera, which when held down enables the user to zoom in or pan out. Some of these cameras have extremely powerful zoom lenses with good quality optics, but care should be taken when zooming in, as even the smallest movement of the camera will be amplified many times. This 'camera shake' can be largely eliminated by the use of a tripod. Ideally one of these should be used as often as possible, but if undertaking field work outside this may prove to be extremely difficult. When panning – that is, moving the camera to follow any action – the user must not move the camera too quickly, as this will make the footage appear blurred and be uncomfortable for the viewer to watch.

There is no need to teach the children how to use the camera, or indeed the techniques of film-making; indeed, let them go and work it out for themselves! It is this experimentation that allows the most effective learning – and as it is all part of digital technology, any mistakes can be immediately erased, with no cost to anybody! However, with younger children it might be helpful to provide some help cards, perhaps with images of the key buttons rather than text.

Step 2   Capturing video

This is the easy bit! As can be seen from the above, it really is just a matter of pointing and shooting. With time, more advanced film-making techniques can be introduced, but initially this will involve techniques that simply make the film bearable to watch, such as not moving the camera too quickly! With some experience the children will start to consider aspects such as where to position themselves, cutaways (where the same action is filmed from different angles), and high and low angle shots. It is also important to frame the subject properly, so that the action is in the middle of the screen, and not so small that it cannot be seen properly or so large that it doesn't all fit in. The person using the camera also needs to ensure that the light source is behind them – in a school hall, for example, if there is strong sunlight from outside there is a possibility that the people being videoed will appear as silhouettes.

The user will be able to see what they are recording, as they can watch it on the camera's built in foldaway screen. However, as with digital 'still' cameras, these should be used sparingly if operating on battery, as they are a very large drain on battery power. A more traditional viewfinder is also provided, but when working indoors it might be better to use mains power (taking care not to trip over the lead), or perhaps to have several spare, fully-charged batteries ready.

As we have already mentioned, this is the same viewfinder that allows immediate playback of any captured footage. The user should ensure that each clip only lasts a few seconds – most television programmes and films only dwell on the action for this amount of time. Another important reason for this is that the editing software automatically cuts the footage up when downloading at the points where the camera is turned on and off, so short clips will help to make editing easier.

Step 3 Downloading the video

Once the required video footage has been captured, the next step is to download it to a computer in readiness for editing. This is important, for like any data that is collected, it has no real meaning until processed by the computer and turned into information. It is highly likely that much more footage will have been captured than can possibly be used or needed, so it will have to be edited to include the important points, rather than absolutely everything. It might also need finishing with sound, music and titles.

There are several very good digital video editing packages, which are very cheap to buy and easy to use. Indeed, iMovie comes free with all Apple computers as part of the Mac operating system, and Windows Movie Maker is supplied free with the Windows XP operating system. As both operating systems are provided as standard on the vast majority of new and modern computers, most people have access to this type of software. Slightly more sophisticated is Pinnacle Studio, which is just as easy to use but has more functions and allows greater flexibility.

Downloading is done with most cameras by connecting them to a computer via a Firewire connection. This is similar to USB, but allows much quicker transmission of data. This is particularly important with digital video; these files are huge, and it only takes a few short videos to completely fill an average-sized hard drive. Consequently, it is preferable to store completed videos on external media such as a CD or DVD rather than on the computer. The captured video is downloaded in real time: that is, if ten minutes of video is captured then it will take ten minutes to download. This is why it is important to record footage in short clips, rather than longer ones. Once the footage has been downloaded it can be edited.

Step 4 Editing the video

This is the point at which the children can be creative for a second time. They will already have had the opportunity for this when they captured the video in the first place, but now they can refine and enhance their work.

Once the video clips have been downloaded into the program, they can be edited by dragging them onto the storyboard at the bottom of the screen. As the video downloads, each individual clip should appear in separate frames on the storyboard. They can then be picked up and dragged along the storyboard, thus removing, copying and re-sequencing clips in the film, in much the same way that text can be edited in a word processing package. By selecting the 'Video effects' option from the 'Tools' menu at the top of the screen, the user can add different effects or transitions between clips. Titles and credits can also be added at this point.

The editing mode can be switched from 'Storyboard' to 'Timeline' mode. The user will then have a visual representation of not only the clips, but also transitions, audio and music tracks and titles. To toggle between the two modes, the user clicks on the 'Show storyboard' button.

Step 5   Finishing the video

Once the children have finished editing their video, they need to decide which format their work should be saved in and then go through a process called rendering. This is where the video footage and all of the component parts such as the titles, audio and music tracks and transitions are saved in one of several possible formats and are 'finished', so all of the separate parts become part of the 'film'. The format chosen will depend on several factors, such as what quality is acceptable, and what media player the pupils have on their computers. For example, if the pupils want a high quality video, where there is the highest video definition and maximum sound quality, then this will take longer to render and save, and will correspondingly use up a large amount of memory. However, if quality is not so important then a lower resolution can be selected, which will take less time to save and render and will take up less memory.

A good tip is always to save the movie before rendering – that way the same 'raw' footage can be used and saved in different formats as often as required, and of course can then be re-edited any number of times. It can be saved onto a recordable CD which can then be viewed on a computer. It can also be saved and sent as an email attachment, saved ready for posting to the Internet or even sent to a digital video camera. Some digital video-editing packages also allow the user to burn the film to a DVD, which can then be played in a DVD player and viewed on a television.

Step 6   Using the finished video

Clearly, digital video is an extremely flexible medium, which enables the children to video their own work and play it back immediately, allowing them to reflect upon and analyse their own work quickly and thoroughly. Alternatively, they can make a film of sequences of movement to play at a class assembly or a school open evening, where the focus is on presentation rather than analysis. A particularly imaginative use of digital video footage is to insert clips into PowerPoint presentations. For example, the teacher (or indeed the children) could produce a plan of the school hall, with the apparatus set up in appropriate positions. Drawn using the 'Draw' and 'AutoShapes' tools (we explain how to do this in Chapter 2), these are then turned into hyperlinked objects. Then they are linked to an appropriate video clip, which is automatically run when the piece of apparatus is clicked on. The video clip might involve children demonstrating how the apparatus should be used correctly. This could be used as a teaching aid before the lesson or even during the lesson, if a laptop computer is taken into the hall.

One of the main advantages of using digital video is that video analysis, which is now a feature of coaching in professional sports such as cricket, can be utilized in the primary school. The same techniques of analysis that are applied to the England cricket team and their academy for younger players are now available during the primary school games lesson. This has the potential to revolutionize the way that sport is taught in our schools. Indeed, with the 2012 Olympic Games approaching, this could make a significant impact in the coming years. Children can perform a sporting action or gymnastic movement, and this can be played back and used as the basis of a teaching aid. It can be shown at normal speed, slowed down or speeded up as appropriate or paused to highlight key points. Getting the maximum advantage out of this is of course also dependent upon the knowledge of the teacher, but certainly this is an excellent starting point. As we have mentioned before, focused questioning is important here: the teacher needs to engage with the pupils in a focused dialogue.

While on the subject of videoing children as part of their work, we need to mention that there are child protection issues to consider. The teacher will need to get permission from the parents before videoing the children, otherwise this cannot take place. Once permission has been given care needs to be taken to ensure that the pupils are appropriately dressed, that filming is for a specific purpose, that the clips will be securely stored and that there is control over who has access to those clips. Once these have been considered and acted upon, the use of digital video can prove to be a great advantage indeed.

Interactive whiteboards

We have already discussed these at length elsewhere in the book, but again, they have a use in PE. For example, when using in 'Annotate over windows' mode, images can be shown on the board of movement or sporting skills being demonstrated, and drawn over with the electronic pens. Another feature is the ability to call up a background screen or tile of a range of courts and pitches, such as a football pitch (Figure 8.1), rugby and hockey pitches and courts for basketball, tennis, netball and handball.

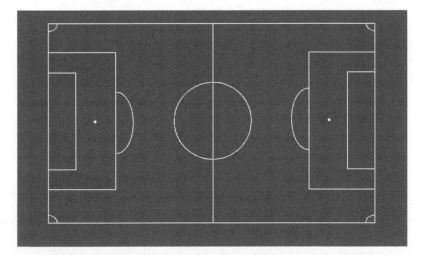

Figure 8.1 A football pitch tile or background screen as provided with the Promethean Activboard. Using the 'Annotate over windows' option, the teacher or the pupils can mark players on the board and drag them around the team to discuss tactics such as marking and finding space. A range of clip art is also provided, including images of people playing a wide range of sports.

CD-Roms

There are some CD-Roms available that can prove useful in the teaching of PE. These include material that contains a range of high quality performances in all aspects of PE and games delivered by professional dancers, gymnasts and sportsmen and women. Other valuable CD-Roms include the BBC Science Simulations 1 and 2, particularly the parts on 'Exercise' and 'Health'. This is closely linked to the QCA Schemes of Work.

Indeed, it seems that the most advantageous use of this aspect of ICT in PE is when it is linked to other subjects. Much of the work we have described in the Music chapter can be linked to 'Music and Movement', while there are many opportunities to include PE in a Science topic mainly concerning the effects of exercise on pulse rates and reaction times. Such an example is described in our book *ICT and Primary Science*, which also includes a case study where the children concerned used this as a practical activity for the National Curriculum requirement, 'Life Processes and Living Things'.

Box 8.1 Some observations on the pulse rate and reaction time topics

These projects were first described by the authors as part of inter-disciplinary Science topics closely connected with PE. However, there is no reason why this situation cannot be reversed, particularly in the light of the current concerns about children's diet and general fitness. Before we concern ourselves with detail, we must emphasize that we have no wish to label children in any way as fit or unfit, and therefore this work needs to be carried out in a sensitive and sympathetic manner. The projects are part of the educational curriculum. If children decide to quietly draw their own conclusions and act upon them, then that is a bonus, but it should not be the main aim.

Pulse rates

Even if these topics are being carried out as part of the PE lesson, the teacher needs to be aware of the scientific processes involved, otherwise the resultant data may well be meaningless. The project is essentially on 'fair tests'. In other words, all tests must be similar in type, carried out in the same way and, from a statistical point of view, in sufficient numbers. For example, we take the pulse rates of the children (and indeed adults) for a purpose. In this case it is to see how soon after exercise the rates return to normal. Therefore we must first take the pulse rate at rest: that is, before the exercise. The exercise need not be a long one – a little skipping will do. The pulse rate is then taken immediately the exercise stops. It is taken a third time after five minutes. In general the fitter the person the more quickly the pulse rate returns to normal. This procedure needs only to be done once with each child.

Reaction rates

This may take longer, but does not have to be done during an actual PE lesson. We like to call it 'Dropping the Ruler'. One child holds one end of a ruler (preferably 30 centimetres long) and places the other end between the open thumb and forefinger of their neighbour. The child holding the ruler then drops it without warning and the second child must catch it. The reaction 'time' is the reading on the ruler at the place where it is caught – if it is. To make the test fair and relevant it should be done ten times, the ruler should of course be held in exactly the same place every time (preferably at the zero point), and there should be no trial runs!

The use of ICT in these projects

Spreadsheet programs are invaluable in projects of this kind, and we have described them in some detail in the Geography chapter. All the information can be listed and collated, and where necessary various calculations can be made. For example, all the ten readings from the reaction project can be listed in the relevant boxes, and an average taken. It is this average reading that is the all-important factor. Most children will naturally improve their performance as the dropping tests progress: however, some will have occasionally missed the ruler altogether. For the test to be fair these misses will still need to be included in the ten drops, but cannot of course be included in the results (for recording purposes, 'Miss' could be entered in the appropriate box).

With the ruler held at the zero point, examples of these readings could therefore be –

- 27, 29, 23, 26, 28, 21, 26, 22, 29, 26. Simple Average – 25.7.
- Miss, 3, 5, 9, Miss, 5, 6, 4, 11, 12. Simple Average – 5.5.

This is an example of how PE can be used to motivate children in a practical way to become interested in a variety of other subjects, in this case Science, Mathematics and of course ICT. An additional teaching point here is that as with so many more less interesting academic tests, the higher the average the better the result!

References

Williams, J. and Easingwood, N. (2003) *ICT and Primary Science.* RoutledgeFalmer, London.

Useful Addresses

BBC Science Simulations 1 and 2 can be obtained through AVP, School Hill Centre, Chepstow, Monmouthshire, NP16 5PH.

Index